UN GRAND BORDEL

First edition, published in 2001 by

WOODFIELD PUBLISHING
Woodfield House, Babsham Lane, Bognor Regis
West Sussex PO21 5EL, England.

© Norman Lee & Eric Geoffrey French, 2001

All rights reserved.
No part of this publication may be reproduced
or transmitted in any form or by any means,
electronic or mechanical, nor may it be stored
in any information storage and retrieval system,
without prior permission from the publisher.

The right of Norman Lee & Eric Geoffrey French
to be identified as the authors of this work
has been asserted by them in accordance with
the Copyright, Designs and Patents Act 1988

ISBN 1 903953 00 6

Un Grand Bordel

*A RAF Airgunner's Experiences
with Bomber Command and
the French Maquis 1943/44*

NORMAN LEE &
GEOFFREY FRENCH

Woodfield Publishing
~WEST SUSSEX • ENGLAND~

Sgt Norman Lee while on active service as an Air Gunner with RAF Bomber Command, 1943.

"The war looked different from the ranks"
(Private Frank Richards in *Old Soldiers Never Die*)

Contents

	Authors' Notes 9
I	Getting In 13
II	Training 21
III	Operations 33
IV	Shot Down 53
V	Evasion 69
VI	Meeting the Duke 89
VII	"Un Grand Bordel" 103
VIII	Winter 123
IX	Spring 137
X	Break-Up 151
XI	Apéritifs and Eau De Vie 167
XII	Into the War Again 183
	Postscript *205*
	Operations Flown by Norman Lee, 1943 ..... *209*
	Some General Comments *215*

AUTHORS' NOTES

Books of war memoirs always interest me, but sometimes I find it difficult to recognise the Royal Air Force, and in particular the Bomber Command that I knew, described in them. Nor have the warriors by or about whom these books are written struck much of a chord of recognition as far as I am concerned. Not that such memoirs are untrue, of course, only untypical. Heroic figures such as Leonard Cheshire and Guy Gibson were rare. They saw more action than most; they took untypical parts in untypical operations; they possessed untypical skill; they were untypically brave.

Now I did not, had not and was not any of these things. I was an ordinary young man of my generation. By definition, therefore, I was probably more typical of the sixty thousand or so aircrew who passed through the ranks of Bomber Command during the Second World War than what I may call the 'upper crust' of extraordinary people by or about whom most of the books are written. I belonged, if you like, to the 'lower crust'. My averageness is emphasised by the fact that my operational life of about six weeks, excluding leave, was about the normal expectation of Bomber Command aircrew in 1943, and that I was shot down on my seventeenth operation, just over halfway through my tour.

Moreover, I never received a decoration – which, again by definition, represents an average achievement. True enough, I was told that if the letter given me by the

American OSS captain under whom I served in my last few weeks in France had been on official notepaper, I would have got a medal. Not that I minded not getting one: I was thankful enough to have returned home in one piece. Besides, I reckon I had a good war and know very well that people who had a far worse one never got within smelling distance of being decorated.

Again, I was not unique in having evaded capture after being shot down, or even in having spent the best part of a year serving in the French Maquis and the American OSS. Although I have often remarked "I could write a book about it", I have always assumed that one of the others better qualified than I would do it. But no one ever did, as far as I know, so when Geoffrey French offered to write up my story if I supplied the information, the opportunity seemed too good to miss. So I talked while he tape-recorded, wrote and edited. Here is the result.

Norman Lee

Norman Lee undersells himself. His sturdy assertion of his 'averageness' as an aircrew member of Bomber Command may be valid enough as far as it goes, but paradoxically that makes his account of both his training and flying operations the more interesting as typifying the war experience of many, many other young men, possibly 'average', but certainly brave.

Over and above this, though, his subsequent career with the French Maquis and the American OSS can hardly be regarded as 'average', if only because it was not given to many members of the Royal Air Force to spend many months of active service clad in German uniform, followed by a shorter period masquerading, and fighting, as an American GI.

The part of the manuscript dealing with flying operations was checked for technical accuracy by Wing Commander W.E. McCrea, DFC, BSc, a former Bomber Command pilot who was completing a tour of operations at about the same time as Norman Lee was starting his. Wing Commander McCrea remarked that this was the only authentic account he had ever seen of Bomber Command operations *as he himself also experienced them*, and of the motives and emotions of those who took part.

Total accuracy of recall cannot be claimed, at this distance of time, for conversations here set down in the direct form. Nor would any purpose be served by reproducing all the hesitations and misunderstandings caused by language difficulties. Some names and nicknames of individuals have been altered or omitted. There is, in addition, some uncertainty about place-names, for reasons explained in the narrative.

Geoffrey French

I

Getting In

Practically the first order I received in the Royal Air Force was "Down slacks, up shirts!" This was at RAF Padgate, where the rituals to which newly-arrived recruits were subjected included a ceremony known as an FFI or 'free from infection' medical examination. We were lined up in a hangar facing the open side, with only a sheet of hessian as a very inadequate screen between us and a crowd of WAAFs who giggled and made faces through the windows of a low building opposite. To complete our embarrassment, as soon as the inspection was over we were marched straight into that self-same building: it was the airmen's mess, and the female spectators who had thus mocked our discomfiture were members of the staff.

The plateful of gristly brawn which was dished out for dinner did little to restore my enthusiasm for my new vocation; indeed, I was beginning to wonder whether I would not have done better to accept the offer I had had a year before of a job in the drawing office of an engineering firm, which would have exempted me from war service altogether.

But that had been in November 1940, when the whole nation was inspired by Dunkirk, the Battle of Britain and

Winston Churchill. At 19 years old, with a twin brother who had already volunteered for aircrew and been accepted, it was not surprising that I wanted to follow his example. Besides, reserved occupation or not, I was afraid that if I didn't join up as aircrew pretty quickly, I might finish up being conscripted into the Army, which didn't interest me then and has never done so since.

My mother, of course, wanted me to take the engineering job, but my father simply said in Yorkshire fashion, "You just do what you think is right, lad; it's up to you." So I reported to the Aircrew Selection Centre at Cardington in February 1941 and was accepted, like my brother before me, as a wireless operator/air gunner, or WOP/AG as we used to say in those days.

It was a bit of an anti-climax when I was sent home from the Selection Centre on indefinite unpaid leave. I imagine that at this comparatively early stage of the war there were more people waiting for training than the existing facilities could cope with. So until my turn came to go through the pipeline I went home and continued with my job as apprentice to an architect and surveyor in Bradford. Not until the middle of November 1941, a year after I had volunteered, did I receive a letter from the Air Ministry. It said I hadn't been forgotten but I wouldn't be called forward for training until at least March 1942. Two weeks later, naturally, my calling-up papers arrived.

Now here I was at RAF Padgate, where the only memorable events, apart from the embarrassment of the FFI, were being kitted out with hairy RAF uniforms – they haven't changed much since then – and discovering that the old, old joke is based on fact: we really were asked if any of us were mechanically-minded, and when my next-door neighbour answered yes for both of us, we were promptly sent to the kitchen to wash plates.

From Padgate we were despatched to Blackpool for basic training. We were placed in civilian billets in Hornby Road, at the back of Central Station. These were boarding-houses and private hotels that had been taken over by the Air Force; in fact Blackpool was just like a huge RAF station in those days. Some of the billets were good and some were bad, and no doubt the same applied to the airmen. Our particular landlady was really goodhearted, despite the hammering her furniture and carpets got from fish and chips being parked on the piano and our great hefty boots clopping all over the house. Those of us who showed a bit of consideration got well dug in, and the landlady would let us come in the back to drink a cup of tea and listen to the wireless.

I started the wireless operators' course and got up to about twelve words a minute. Now learning Morse is like learning to play a musical instrument: either you get the knack or you don't. I didn't. Mind you, the school was in the tramsheds, it was mid-winter, and naturally there was no heating, so the conditions were far from ideal. However that may be, I couldn't manage more than twelve words a minute no matter what I did. They used to give us a test every Thursday in a big hall above Burton's shop on the Promenade. I have always believed that this was how the Air Force expression 'going for a Burton' originated, because after failing this test three weeks running I was taken off the course.

An officer interviewed me and asked, "What do you want to be?"

"An air gunner, sir," I said.

He looked at the piece of paper in front of him and grunted.

"Well," he said, "I can tell you this. Your results have got worse and worse every week. In the first week you only failed by one error, but now you've got to the point where I can scarcely find anything that you've done right, so if you think you're going to be an air gunner you're sadly mistaken, because I shall personally see to it that you don't get there."

Despite this threat, I was soon accepted for training as a 'straight AG' – in other words, an air gunner pure and simple, without the Morse requirement. This was the end of Blackpool for me, and I was shipped off to Kirton-on-Lindsey in Lincolnshire to await a vacancy on a training course. Here I became a general labourer and odd-job man, sweeping roads, picking up paper, painting kerbstones... the traditional routine for anyone the Services don't know what to do with.

I finished up emptying dustbins, which was an exceptionally good job. The normal working week in wartime was seven days, but dustbin emptying was supposed to be particularly arduous, so we only had a five and a half-day week. The wagon we used was a big old civilian removal van with its floor four feet off the ground, so it was indeed quite hard work humping dustbins on and off it. But we had special clothing, plenty of scrounges and extra time off (much more than those in authority ever knew) so we reckoned we were well looked after. Emptying dustbins was a bloody good job in the war!

Unfortunately, it did not last long as far as I was concerned. One day I found myself attached to an aircraft servicing flight, allegedly to receive some sort of training, but actually to perform minor clerical tasks. When this servicing flight was moved to Northolt, I went with it, and from there was summoned to Weston-super-Mare one day to appear before a 'board'. This consisted of three officers, including a flight lieutenant air gunner who was rather hard of hearing but didn't seem to know it. After a bit of preliminary sparring he suddenly asked, "Now then, Lee, what do you say to going on a pilot's course, hey? How'd you like to be a pilot?"

This rocked me back on my heels. Not only was it unexpected, but to be a pilot was the last thing I wanted. My twin brother, who had also failed the wireless operator's course, was now under training as a straight AG and I was on fire to catch up with him.

"Well sir," I hedged, "I haven't exactly thought about it. If I..."

"Speak up, lad!" the flight lieutenant interrupted, "we can't hear you if you mumble like that!"

I raised my voice.

"I said I haven't thought about it very much."

"Not thought about it? Not thought about it? Should have thought every young fellow these days must have *thought* about it. Why don't you want to be a pilot?"

I became nervous. It looked as though the board was not going to look very favourably on a chap who didn't want to be a pilot.

"I didn't mean I don't *want* to be a pilot," I said. "I've just never imagined myself as one. I suppose being a fighter pilot might be all right."

"Eh, what's that?" he asked, frowning and cupping his hand over his ear.

"I might like to be a fighter pilot," I bawled.

"All right, all right, you don't have to shout at me, I'm not deaf," he said irritably, and threw down his pen. He glared at me accusingly and went on. "So you'd like to be a fighter pilot. Why not a bomber pilot, eh? What's wrong with being a bomber pilot?"

The truth was, I didn't want to be any sort of a pilot, because a pilot's training took about eighteen months compared with six weeks for a straight AG. I wanted to get operational, and to become a straight AG was the fastest way of doing it. But I was so intimidated by the board's seeming insistence on my training as a pilot that I didn't have the sense to tell them the truth. I plunged on desperately, saying the first thing that came into my head.

"Well, you see, as a bomber pilot I'd be responsible for the lives of the rest of the crew as well as my own. As a fighter pilot, if I did anything silly the only one killed would be myself."

There was a heavy silence as the three officers looked at one another. At last the deaf flight lieutenant spoke again.

"Is that what you really think?" he asked.

"Yes," I said rather doubtfully, for I could see something was going badly wrong.

"And what about being an air gunner? To start with you said that's what you wanted to be. Don't you understand that an air gunner on a bomber crew has some responsibility? It's not only the pilot who has people's lives in his hands, you know. The same applies to every member of the crew, and since you don't seem to realise that, I doubt whether you ought to be on the aircrew list at all."

It didn't take the other officers long, in fact, to agree with him, and when I got back to Northolt I was given the choice of remustering to a ground trade or accepting my discharge. The latter, I was very pointedly told, would mean that I'd be in the Army within 24 hours.

So that was it. I applied to remuster as an ACH/GD (Aircraft Hand General Duties). This was just about the same as a general labourer, a kind of mugabout who did all the mucky jobs, but it looked like the best bet because they promised immediate promotion to LAC (Leading Aircraftman) which meant a few coppers a week more pay.

I had the last laugh, however, because a few days later an entry appeared in Station Routine Orders calling for volunteers to train as air gunners. I went to the orderly room as fast as my legs would carry me, kept my face straight while they did the paperwork, and within a fortnight received orders to report to St John's Wood in London for a medical examination and issue of flying clothing. From there, in company with 30 other prospective air gunners, I took the train for Bridlington and the Elementary Air Gunnery Training Course. I was 'in' at last!

Norman Lee during training.

II

Training

The CO of the Elementary Air Gunnery School at Bridlington was an ex-fighter pilot from the 1914-18 war. He'd rejoined as a flight lieutenant and was a real good stick. He would drop into our billets of an evening for a chat and if he found us sitting without a fire would organise a raid on the nearest RAF coal and coke compound, using the boot of his car to carry off the loot.

Less popular with us was our corporal drill instructor, an ex-Guardsman who, we soon noticed, always dismissed us for our morning and afternoon breaks outside the same café. One day he marched us there as usual and went inside (for his 'kickback' we assumed). Without waiting to be dismissed we scooted to another café for our cups of tea, arriving back in front of the usual place at the proper time. Naturally, the corporal was furious and laid charges against us for dismissing ourselves without authority; naturally the CO found us guilty. Our punishment, however, was to tidy up the CO's office that evening, and there, thoughtfully laid out on the desk, we found the draft notes with our postings to the Air Gunnery School.

The Bridlington course had been very good value. We did aircraft recognition, weapons familiarisation, clay-pigeon shooting (believe it or not) and Aldis lamp and

Morse code up to ten words a minute. The latter surprised me a bit, but even straight air gunners had to do this much, so as to be able to read airfield beacons.

We had been told that the Bridlington course would exempt us from the pre-flying element of the course at the Air Gunnery School at Pembrey, near Llanelly in South Wales. Nothing of the sort happened, however, and despite our protests that we knew the sighting procedures inside out and could strip and reassemble a Browning machine-gun in our sleep, we went back to square one and did the preliminary training all over again. The reason was simple. A training backlog had built up because of bad weather and the Bridlington pre-course, although excellent, had been devised merely to keep us occupied while awaiting our turn at Pembrey.

I started actual flying at last on 1st April 1943, over two years after joining up and 25 years to the day, incidentally, from the amalgamation of the old Royal Flying Corps and Royal Naval Air Service to form the Royal Air Force. My first flight was in a Blenheim, an aircraft type which I shall always remember because of the fancy seat-mechanism in the gunner's turret.

The idea was that when the gunner rose to lower the guns the seat would rise with him and when he raised them, the seat would drop. This never worked. When you stood up to depress the guns, the seat would arrive two or three seconds later and give you a thump in the behind, just as you were about to fire, and when you raised the guns it would wait until you'd got everything lined up, then suddenly collapse under you.

Our firing practice was done out at sea, against drogues towed by Westland Lysander aircraft. There would be three of us trainee gunners in the Blenheim, and we would be allowed a hundred practice rounds each. The bullets were painted three different colours – red, blue and yellow, I think – so that you knew which of the three gunners had fired the various rounds. The Lysander used to come at us from various angles, according to the sort of shooting we were supposed to be practising. There was no great danger for the Lysander, because the towline to the drogue was pretty long, but on occasion, oddly enough, it could be dangerous for the Blenheim from which the firing took place.

The source of the trouble was the foot-pedal we could depress if we wanted to increase the area the guns could sweep. This gave us another five degrees to port or starboard. The device worked well enough if the target was on the beam, but if the Lysander was doing what we called a 'quarter-crossover', where it started on one side and swung underneath to the other, it was quite possible for the gunner to shoot his own aircraft's tail off.

It would happen this way... In normal operation, when you swung the gun round through the arc of your tail, there was a cam surface which made the guns swing up and over. However, if you had depressed the foot-pedal and didn't release it again, the cam surface didn't work until it was too late. I knew of at least one instance where a training aircraft returned to base with a self-perforated tail assembly.

There was one other disconcerting feature associated with this foot-pedal too. If you didn't take your foot off smartly enough, the guns were liable to carry on swinging until they squashed your head against the perspex side of the turret.

My old logbook shows that my highest score was nine per cent hits, and on a good few occasions I didn't score any hits at all. This was pretty common: there were plenty of other trainees just as bad. Furthermore, there were many times when either the guns or the aircraft or both would be U/S: in my own case, out of thirteen training flights the guns were U/S three times. On a fourth occasion there was insufficient time for me to do my firing. This often happened if you were third to fire.

Despite all this, I passed out with 77 per cent in the final exam and flying hours of 15 hours and 20 minutes. My final shooting average was 2.4 per cent and for this I received on my report the comments:

> *"A hardworking cadet who has got high marks; should make a good air gunner and NCO."*
>
> *"Minimum air firing not completed owing to unfavourable weather."*

To be frank, I reckon they were not too particular at this period of the war as to whether you completed absolutely the whole of your firing and flying; the main thing was to get you operational. They needed air gunners and there was a backlog of volunteers waiting so they passed us out smartly from the course.

At the beginning of May 1943 we were sent to 24 OTU at Honeybourne, near Stratford on Avon, for 'crewing up'.

The crewing-up procedure was like a casual proposal of marriage. When we arrived, we were all paraded and the pilots walked down the ranks. If they liked the look of you they would ask: "Would you be my air gunner?" Since there weren't enough air gunners to go round, rear gunners only were allocated at first, mid-upper gunners joining later on.

I was lucky. My pilot, Johnny Harkins, was a Scotsman about 35 years old who had previously been in the Army. He had been evacuated from Dunkirk with the 51st Highland Division, one of the few who got back, the Division having been annihilated at St Valéry. He had transferred to the RAF as a pilot and for two years had been a flying instructor and staff pilot on training courses, so I certainly had a boss with plenty of experience. We were an all-NCO crew, all the others having already joined, except for the mid-upper gunner.

Alec Parkinson, the wireless operator, came from Blackburn. He was our other 'old man', being in his thirties, and was the only married member of the crew. The rest of us were about nineteen or twenty. 'Stan' Baldwin, the bomb aimer, came from somewhere near Stratford on Avon, where he had been brought up by a couple of maiden aunts, though to meet him you would never have believed this. The navigator was Don Richards, from Sevenoaks. Alec Scott, inevitably known as 'Scotty', came from Scotland, appropriately enough (Stornoway, in fact); he was our flight engineer. The mid-upper gunner, who joined us later, was a Canadian, Sergeant Columbus, whom we naturally called 'Chris'. So we were quite a mixed bunch. Despite this, or perhaps because of it, we settled down very well together.

After crewing up we stayed on at Honeybourne for a week's ground course of dinghy drill and things of that nature. The air gunners did the usual aircraft recognition, turret familiarisation and clearing of stoppages. After this we moved to Long Marston, where we did some flying in Whitleys. This was more for the pilot than anyone else. He flew dual with a staff pilot, circuits, landings and so on, until he was considered capable of taking it on his own. Then we did cross-country flights, navigation exercises, night flying, bombing runs and so forth. There was very little for me to do during this time except just sit, practising the procedures I was suppose to adopt in case of attack by enemy aircraft. We had a bit of excitement one night when we found ourselves over Hull during a German air raid. It came as a shock at this stage of our training, and we got out of it pretty smartly.

On another occasion we were on a cross-country flight when I suddenly spotted a great length of wire dangling out behind us. It was just typical of the Whitley that the intercom was U/S at the time. I crawled from the turret up the fuselage, tapped the wireless operator on the shoulder and told him about it. I went back to my turret, and the pilot turned into a civilian airfield nearby. As we entered the circuit I noticed this wire vanishing. Of course it rang a bell then: it was the wireless operator's trailing aerial, which he used to wind out during flight. But by that time we had our wheels down ready for landing, so I couldn't tell Johnny it was a false alarm. However, as soon as we came to a stop I went up front and told Alec, "It's your damned trailing aerial!" Johnny was certainly a fast thinker: when the ground staff came out he said his ailerons were a bit stiff or something, and would they try to ease them? So our face was saved.

During this course, which lasted from 7 May to 20 June, we were joined by Chris, our Canadian mid-upper gunner. He got about twice as much pay as I did for doing exactly the same job. There was another thing too. Any Canadian who completed ten operations was automatically put up for a commission. But despite these differences, which were not Chris' fault, we got on very well together, as indeed did the whole crew.

For me personally, the most important event of the course was a telegram from home telling me that my twin brother was missing. The Lancaster in which he was rear gunner had failed to return from a raid on Wilhelmshaven. I went home on compassionate leave. My mother tried to persuade me to stop flying, but of course I refused. She never really forgave me for this, almost up to the time she died, nor did she like it when I decided to stay in the Air Force after the war. My father took the customary masculine attitude: if I wanted to continue flying, it was up to me.

I never had the slightest doubt about wanting to fly. Although I felt deeply about my brother's death, it never occurred to me not to go on flying – rather the reverse. I wanted to get my own back and the way to do this was to get my training finished and get operational. This had been my whole idea in joining as an air gunner in the first place: it was the quickest of the aircrew courses. I had been decidedly unlucky that it had taken me so long to start flying. So my brother's death only reinforced my determination. It may all sound a bit crude and unreal now, but I was only twenty and that was the way people thought in wartime.

Oddly enough, I can't say that I ever much enjoyed the flying itself. The alleged poetry and beauty of it left me cold and still does. Going on an op in an aeroplane was just riding to work as far as I was concerned – quicker and less tiring than walking and that's all there was to it. Admittedly, I did join aircrew partly because of the glamour attached to it, and I think a lot of others did the same, but I never thought of flying as glamorous; it was just other people, who weren't aircrew, that did. Of course it was wartime and everybody had to do something, and I think I've already made it clear that I didn't fancy being an infantryman. To put it plainly, aircrew was the most comfortable job I could think of in which you were doing something worthwhile.

The swank was certainly enjoyable. During training we had a white flash in our headgear, and like most other aircrew trainees I was very proud to wear this. It set us apart from anyone else in the Forces. When we passed out from the AGS we took down the white flashes and got our tapes and air gunner's brevet instead. We were proud of being in the Royal Air Force, proud of being aircrew, and proud of walking down the street with people sneaking admiring or envious glances at us.

Mind you, I realise that not everyone would have wanted to be aircrew. I have heard infantrymen say they wouldn't fly for a king's ransom. But in my opinion the infantrymen had a much worse job than ours. We didn't have to creep about in ditches with rain dripping down our necks and bullets whizzing about our ears. We just flew, and then came back to a nice warm bed.

We were privileged in other ways too. Unlike other airmen we had sheets on our beds even when we were under training. Bacon and egg, a tremendous luxury in wartime, was the standard 'flying meal'. We also got orange juice, chocolate and chewing gum when we were flying. It wasn't just these items themselves that we appreciated: it was the fact that we had them when other people didn't that gave us status, made us feel that we were somebody. And we'd have been blind not to notice that people did respect us, Service people and civilians too.

I have often been asked since the war what I felt about all the other aircrew being killed on operations. Of course we were aware of the danger – I believe that there were periods during the war when the average life expectancy of an air gunner on operations was about six weeks – but I can't say that I thought about it much at the time. I can't explain this. Courage didn't come into it. I see courage as something that happens in response to immediate danger. It just didn't seem to have anything to do with me. Mind you, I've always been renowned for my lack of imagination and I've never been in the habit of worrying about the future either. I don't know whether my attitude was typical, but certainly it seems to have been well suited to my situation at that time.

It wasn't only on ops that aircrew got killed. Quite a few lost their lives during training, but this didn't bother me either. However, I must admit to one slightly eerie incident that occurred when I was waiting to go on leave immediately after we had finished at the OTU.

I was asked to join another crew, who were short-handed, for a trip in a Whitley. Strictly speaking, aircrew always had to fly when ordered, but in practice reluctance to make a training flight with a pilot or crew other than your own was generally handled sympathetically. On this occasion, I was reluctant. They pressed me, but I stayed obstinate. I'd been sticking my neck out in these old Whitleys for long enough and I wasn't going to do it any more. I just didn't want to fly, and no one was going to make me. So they put the bomb aimer in the turret because they were a gunner short. The aircraft crashed on take-off. No one was hurt except the bomb aimer. He was killed.

Far from upsetting me, this incident seemed to me to prove I was right in backing my own judgment, and I went off on leave quite happily.

We next reported to No 1659 Conversion Unit at Topcliffe for yet another course. This was on Halifaxes, so we now knew what kind of aircraft we would be flying on operations. The Halifax was one of the three types of big four-engined bombers that were coming into service at this time. According to the experts it was better than the Stirling but not as good as the Lancaster, but bomber crews cared nothing for experts or statistics: the type you flew in was the best, and to hell with the others!

I can recall only a couple of training trips from this period. On one of them we went round the Isle of Man on a bombing exercise. I didn't properly know how the business worked, and to tell the truth I wasn't all that interested, because on all these trips I was really a passenger. It was the rest of the crew who were being trained when we flew. Most of an air gunner's training took place on the ground: aircraft recognition, stripping guns and so forth. Apart from the few occasions when I fired off my guns, about all I had to do when flying was help the navigator to determine wind-drift. I would line up the sight in the rear turret on an object dead astern, advise the navigator immediately I had done so, then continue swinging the turret to keep the object in the centre of the sight until he told me to stop. Then I would read off the degrees of traverse from a scale marked on the side of the turret. From this the navigator worked out what effect the wind was having on the progress of the flight.

The only memorable feature of this particular trip as far as I was concerned was that when we were coming back from Douglas I asked for my flying rations to be sent down to the turret. Alec, the wireless operator, brought them down, and I sat back peacefully and scoffed them. It wasn't until the pilot asked when I was going to send the sandwiches back for the rest of the crew that I realised I had eaten the rations for seven men!

The last exercise we did was what they used to call 'fighter affiliation'. We were 'attacked' by a Spitfire from one of the squadrons stationed nearby. We then took evasive action. Although done in daylight, it was good practice. The standard manoeuvres were to corkscrew, dive or climb according to the angle from which the fighter made his pass. When I think back I wonder why this sort of thing didn't make me sick, but it didn't. I've only been sick twice when flying, and both times it was when I was sitting up front getting all the engine fumes. (Being sick in the aircraft cost half a crown a go: this was the standard charge made by the ground staff for clearing it up.)

Norman's crew, 1943: *(l to r)*
Back row: *Chris Columbus (mid-upper gunner); Don Richards (navigator); Stan Baldwin (bomb aimer); Alec Scott (flight engineer);*
Front row: *Alec Parkinson (wireless operator); Johnny Harkins (pilot); Norman Lee (rear gunner)*

III

Operations

We finished flying training on 24 July 1943 and were posted to No 428 Squadron, based at Middleton St George, in Yorkshire (now a civil airport). Although we were nominally a Canadian squadron, over half the personnel were RAF, and there was a sprinkling of Australians as well. Of course it sometimes worked the other way round, so that an RAF squadron might contain a large number of Canadians, Australians and New Zealanders.

Before we started ops our pilot had to make two 'second-dickey' trips as co-pilot with an experienced pilot and crew for familiarisation. Our first operation together was on 2nd August 1943, when we were briefed to go to Hamburg. This was in fact the last in the series of 'round-the-clock' raids by ourselves at night and the Americans by day that more or less wiped Hamburg off the map.

Perhaps I ought to say something about my apprehensions, but quite honestly I can't really say that I had any, apart from being a little concerned about the weather. The met people warned us at briefing that we would meet a 'front' as we crossed the North Sea, and we were told we must turn back if it became really bad. The forecast turned out to be only too accurate – it was predictions of good weather that were generally wrong – and we found it impossible to climb over the front as we had been instructed. Lightning was striking the aircraft continuously, blue flames were shooting from the ends of the gun barrels, and the needles of the flying instruments were spinning like tops. Of the 32 aircraft on our station (No 419 Squadron was also based there), I believe only three actually reached Hamburg, and ours was not one of them. But we did get credited with an operation: we managed to reach Heligoland and dropped our bombs there – which was quite a tricky proposition as a matter of fact, since Heligoland was well defended by anti-aircraft guns and searchlights.

However that may be, the weather was so atrocious that the Germans couldn't do much that night except poop off a few rounds, more as a gesture than in real hope, and I doubt whether any night-fighter could have got off the ground. On the whole, I can't say that this first taste of war impressed me very much.

Our next operation wasn't until 9 August, when we went to Mannheim. This was an eight-hour trip, involving about five hours over enemy territory. There was nothing spectacular about it: a few searchlights and a touch of flak, that was all. On 10 August we raided Nuremberg: again an uneventful trip.

By this time we were becoming quite blasé about the whole thing and felt we were a thoroughly experienced crew. I believe this was true of most crews on operations: after the first three or four trips they began to feel fireproof. And as a matter of fact it really seemed as if some crews were. I've spoken to many a flier who got through a complete tour of operations without encountering any trouble at all – no fighters, no flak within miles of them, never caught by searchlights, no narrow squeaks or even a bit of engine trouble, nothing. It depended on your luck. A complete tour was thirty ops, but as far as the crews were concerned this meant 28, the pilot having done his two second-dickey trips previously. It was when you got into the home stretch around 25 ops that you would start sweating. However, our crew was spared this anxiety, because we were shot down before we reached that point.

Our fourth trip was to Milan, a very long one indeed, lasting over ten hours, and it brought a few nervous moments. It got off to a bad start because we didn't take our own navigator. He used to get terribly airsick, so he was sent for a medical check-up and we got a young pilot officer as stand-in. This didn't please us much, not because he was an officer or because we doubted his technical competence (of which we then knew nothing) but because it was unsettling to have a stranger flying with us. Even before take-off I fear that Johnny's efforts, as pilot and captain, to make him feel at home received little or no support from the rest of us.

None of us wanted to go, and we were hoping for foul weather or a dud engine; but we got off all right, and indeed reached Milan without any trouble. It was a beautiful moonlit night, and the Alps were a breathtaking sight. This was the only occasion on which I was impressed by all the grandeur and beauty of flight that people write about (I've never heard anyone *talk* about it). And it was both touching and encouraging to see the V-for-victory torchlight signals flashed at us by the people of the French Alpine villages.

There was hardly any opposition to speak of over Milan. Our bombs added their quota to what was just a big firework display, and then we turned for home. That was when the trouble started.

First of all the wind changed and the navigator got lost. He didn't actually admit this, but there's no doubt he was a long way off track. We ultimately found ourselves over Paris, of all places, and they gave us a dreadful pasting. The searchlights had us coned for about ten minutes while the flak gunners threw everything they had at us. Since we were on our own, we received the undivided attention of the defences. Our luck was in, however, and we got away in the end by flying into thick cloud. As we discovered later to our amazement, the aircraft hadn't received a scratch. I began breathing normally again as the French coast came into sight – and then our stand-in navigator made the astounding suggestion that to get himself on track again we should fly along the French coast until he could locate some prominent landmark and thus identify our position.

Our simultaneous protests at this brilliant idea practically blew up the intercom. Only Johnny, the pilot, kept silent until the hubbub died down, then he made it clear that he had only one intention as far as the French coast was concerned, and that was to let it recede into the distance astern of us as rapidly as possible.

This, by the way, was the only time that our very strong aircraft discipline was broken. In films about the war, the crews seem to chatter away over the intercom all the time about popsies, wizard prangs and all the rest of it, using Christian names and generally giving a rather happy-go-lucky impression. I can assure you our crew never did this. You couldn't have people chiming up any old time they liked with bits of idle gossip, because they might pick on a moment when some other member of the crew had something important to say. And we always followed the correct procedure when we spoke to one another: "Rear gunner to pilot", "Pilot to navigator" and so on. No one was ever addressed by his first name while we were in flight, which was as it should be.

Not long after leaving the French coast we passed a Junkers 88 legging it in the opposite direction, presumably after bombing England. I don't know which of us was the more frightened, but neither he nor we stayed to find out.

In the end we reached England, reorientated ourselves and found our way to Topcliffe. We were so short of petrol that Johnny landed downwind, and two of our engines actually died of thirst just as we finished our landing run. So as the old Duke of Wellington would have said, "It was a damned close-run thing."

It was probably a bit brutal of us, but I don't think anyone spoke a single word to the poor old navigator after we left the aircraft. There was none of that sense of comradeship that is supposed to be generated by sharing and surmounting common dangers. Or rather, that was just the trouble: the comradeship existed, but it was between the regular crew and it didn't include stand-in navigators who lost the way home.

To me, this episode illustrates what I still say to this day about Bomber Command operations: that the most important member of the crew was the navigator. With a good navigator, three quarters of your worries were over. It wasn't only over the target that the flak could catch you, but on the way to or from it as well. If that happened it was probably due to bad navigation, because we were told at the pre-op briefing where the flak concentrations were and how to avoid them. Moreover, if you got on the outskirts of the main bomber stream – and this would be the navigator's fault – you were much more likely to be picked off by night-fighters.

We were also briefed on the direction from which to approach the target. We might be told to bomb on the outward leg, then turn and come home, or alternatively we might have to complete the outward leg and bomb on the way back. The latter was what we normally did and what we preferred, because as soon as the bombs were gone you could put your nose down and go like hell away from the target area. This again was where a good navigator came in, and there's nothing like getting home quick for making a navigator popular.

The pilot, on the other hand, we always used to call the driver, and without any intention to disparage the job, that's what he was. The flight engineer sat beside the pilot and also had the astrodome, from which he helped to keep a look-out for night-fighters. We had a swing arrangement fixed up under the astrodome for him so that he wouldn't have to stand. This collapsed one night when he was using it, and from his language the rest of us thought he must have broken his neck at least. It wasn't as bad as that, but he certainly got a severe shaking.

The bomb aimer used to help the navigator by operating the GEE apparatus and other navigation aids. But often enough this equipment was jammed by the Germans. It used to function all right until we got fifty miles or so inside the French coast, then it would pack up. This is where a good navigator came in again, because shortly after take-off the gunner would help the navigator to find a drift, and that was all we had to work on once the navigation aids were out of action. If the wind suddenly changed and you didn't find out quickly enough, you'd finish up a long way off track.

The bomb aimer also had the job of dropping 'window' – strips of aluminium foil that we dropped by the thousand to saturate the German radar defences. The bomb aimer would chuck bundles of it out through the flare chute at five-minute intervals starting about half an hour before reaching the target. I can't remember that we ever had to drop it when we were coming back; it was always when we were going. Of course the whole idea was to get the bombers there to drop the bombs: perhaps getting us back again was a secondary consideration!

The rear gunner was in an isolated position, of course, away down at the end of the aircraft. The only contact was the intercom, which we weren't allowed to use unless someone asked a question or we were being attacked. You might report flak positions or searchlights, but otherwise it was dead quiet apart from the aircraft noise. I used to sing to myself the whole way there and back. I still do it today when driving my car, except that I don't sing, I whistle. For that matter I did it continually in the office during my much less adventurous administrative career in the postwar Air Force, and I'm told that it's the same old tune over and over again. [He did and it was. I think the (very off-key) tune is *Drink To Me Only With Thine Eyes* but his daughter believes it is *Tiptoe Through The Tulips*. In any event neither song seems very appropriate to the activities it accompanied (EGF)]

My principal job at the back was simply to search and search for night-fighters, never stopping or letting up, and it could get pretty tedious. It was cold in the turret too. I had an electric flying-suit, electric gloves and electric socks inside my flying-boots, and I certainly needed them. In October, for instance, it was quite normal for ice to form on your oxygen mask. It was always said, by the way, that the oxygen helped night vision. I suppose it may have done, by keeping us more awake and therefore more alert. I know the mask was a damned irritation on the face at times, and you had it on the whole way there and back once you got above 9,000 feet.

We used to get flying rations to take with us, but apart from the chewing gum, which we champed at incessantly, we didn't touch them until we reached the English coast again. Then the bomb aimer or flight engineer might come back and relieve me in the turret and I would go up to the rest position for a quick sandwich and a hot drink. One attractive but almost invariably useless item was the tin of orange juice. It was usually frozen solid.

We were always told – and this may be a surprise to some people – that shooting enemy fighters down was not what the rear gunner existed for but bringing the aircraft back. In other words, the vital part of the job was to spot the night-fighters in time for the pilot to take evasive action. Firing your guns at the enemy was only a last resort if you failed to evade him, the point being that when you opened up with your guns you were giving a firework display, so if there was another fighter in the vicinity he would spot it and join in the party. The longest a fighter could expect to stay with you would be two minutes, and once he had made his pass that was the finish. He would never come back simply because he couldn't: there wasn't a chance in a thousand of his ever finding you again. So as I say, the essential thing was to detect him and make yourself scarce.

I believe this policy was being changed about the time we were shot down. This was because we were getting on top of the German defences by then, and so we were developing the idea of shooting down as many night-fighters as possible. But for my own part I never fired my guns in anger, although we did have two brushes with fighters. On the second of these occasions we were shot down. The first happened during an attack on Nuremberg, possibly on 10 August 1943. The town was thoroughly lit up and it was like flying in daylight. This was very lucky, since it enabled me to spot this FW 190 from a good way off, climbing up towards us from behind and slightly to port. On receiving my warning Johnny dived, turning into the enemy, which was the customary evasive action. The theory was that since a fighter was such a small aircraft, the G-force acted upon the pilot much more than it did in a heavy bomber, so you hoped that as he turned he would black out, and by the time he came to you would have vanished. On this particular occasion, as it happened, there was another Halifax flying more or less parallel to the fighter, and the German must have lost sight of us when we dived, or else he may have decided that the other Halifax was an easier target, because he swung over and had a go at it from the beam. When we got back to base we discovered that this Halifax had been one of our own squadron. Nobody had been hurt, but the aircraft was full of holes and the crew had a few choice words to say on learning that we were the aircraft that the FW 190 had turned up his nose at in order to attack them.

The Halifaxes on our squadron had had their upper turrets removed to give better speed, and the so-called mid-upper gunner lay on his stomach in the floor of the aircraft looking downwards through a perspex blister, watching out for attacks from below. We were all for this arrangement, because we knew that most attacks by night-fighters came from that direction, where neither the rear gunner nor the bomb aimer could see. Putting the so-called mid-upper gunner where he could search continuously beneath the aircraft eliminated our one blind spot, and more than outweighed the loss of fire-power occasioned by removing the mid-upper turret.

We had another aid for dodging the night-fighters. The wireless operator had a device for listening in on the German fighter control. As soon as he picked up voices he would couple in a microphone fitted to one of the Halifax's engines and broadcast its roar to them on the same frequency, which undoubtedly must have made it a bit difficult for the Germans to hear one another.

A less successful contraption was the one we christened the panic-box. This was a type of radar, I believe, which made a blipping sound that was supposed to intensify whenever anything approached the aircraft from below. This would give warning of enemy fighters from that quarter. Unfortunately the thing was unable to distinguish between friend and foe. We even suspected it responded simply to bits of high ground that we passed over. In the target area, of course, where there were lots of aircraft, it blipped like fury. It threw us into a state of such continuous and useless consternation that we very quickly restored peace of mind by the only method possible – we switched it off and kept it that way.

There were indeed all kinds of ideas and gadgets for keeping the enemy off our backs and getting home safely, but I still think that the most reliable of them was to do as you were told at briefing. Stick to the recommended course and so dodge the flak; fly at the prescribed height; bomb from the prescribed direction; get to the target on time.

Crews who arrived early or late were apt to please themselves about how to bomb. If early and briefed to bomb going in, they might instead pass over the target and bomb going out. If they were late they might bomb on the run-in, regardless of how they had been briefed. Thus there could be a number of aircraft going in unexpected directions, causing confusion over the target. When you consider the density of traffic at the height of a heavy 'saturation' raid, with anything up to a thousand bombers hitting a town in about twenty minutes, the danger of this kind of thing can be appreciated. There were indeed a good number of collisions. And not only that, but bombs could get dropped on to an aircraft from other bombers above. I have looked up from my rear turret and felt a bit hairy to see an aircraft above us coming in from the opposite direction with its bomb doors open. And a few months later, when I was with the French Resistance, I met up with a flight lieutenant and a warrant officer from my squadron who had been brought down in this way. The bombs from another aircraft went right through their own and wrecked it, though of course without exploding. The rear gunner was furious about it, because he had seen the aircraft above them and had warned his pilot, who happened to be CO of the squadron. It was a nice quiet night with no flak, and there was no reason why the pilot shouldn't have turned off his bombing run and gone round again, but he carried on – with the result as aforesaid.

So if any hopeful young aircrew going on an operation should ever ask me how best to make sure of coming back alive, I'd say this: there are bound to be unpredictable factors, and everyone must play these off the cuff, but at least don't add to them by gratuitous disobedience to orders. In other words, do as you've been told at briefing. Mind you, I'm a fine one to talk, considering how little attention I paid at briefings. But then there wasn't much for a gunner to bother about apart from the odd morsel of information about a night-fighter airfield or a bad flak area. This was why I preferred being a gunner: I didn't have to do any worrying. The other members of the crew had specialist briefings, but the gunners only went to the general one, when the whole crew sat at one table.

Not that everything said at briefings was infallible. For instance the entry of the met man was invariably the cue for groans and hollow laughter: he was regarded as the comedy turn. Whatever he said was greeted with derision, especially if he predicted clear weather.

It wasn't only the weather forecast that could turn out to be a dud either. Our intelligence could occasionally be faulty in other respects too. We found this out when we took part in the raid on the German rocket station at Peenemunde on 17 August. I've never seen it mentioned in anything I've read that other aircraft besides Lancasters were involved, but the fact is that over a third of the force consisted of Halifaxes – and there were some Stirlings too. We thought we saw a Manchester (the twin-engined forerunner of the Lancaster) over the target area, and I believe other crews reported seeing one as well, but Air Ministry records say nothing about Manchesters being used. So either we were mistaken or the Germans had put a captured one up for some mysterious purpose of their own.

Peenemunde was our fifth operation. We had been on ops a fortnight, and now we were veterans. In fact at the rate that we were losing crews in those days we were well on, because you could pretty well guarantee that a couple of aircraft would go missing on every op, and the strength of the squadron was only sixteen. As far as I can remember only eight crews went to Peenemunde from our station, four from each squadron. They only sent the experienced crews – and with four raids under our belts we counted as experienced.

The briefing told us to fly over Denmark and find some island or other (carefully avoiding Swedish air space unless we were going to have to bale out or ditch), then turn and bomb from low level – 5,000 feet, in fact, the lowest level we could bomb from without risking damage to the aircraft itself. We were further told, for good measure, that we'd better make a good job of it, because if we didn't totally wipe out the target we'd be going there again the following night and would continue to do so until not a trace of it was left.

There were three waves went to Peenemunde. The first wave was instructed to obliterate the scientists and their living quarters; the second wave was to attack the workshops and storage installations. We were in the third wave. Our squadron was always finding itself in the last wave, which was a good place for getting clobbered, because by the time we arrived the defences were always blazing away.

Peenemunde was no exception. We had been told at briefing that there would be no fighters, only a few searchlights and very little flak. This was totally untrue. When we reached the target area it was stiff with all three. By the time the third wave arrived they had whistled up the fighters. With the searchlights and flak guns it was different. It was true that the Germans had a lot of these mounted on railway trucks, and they could shunt them about pretty rapidly, particularly in the Ruhr valley, where the towns were bunched close together. But Peenemunde is a bit of an isolated spot and I shouldn't think they were able to bring them up fast enough, so there must have been plenty of flak guns and searchlights already in position, because I can't remember ever seeing such a display before or since.

As a matter of fact, I hate to admit this, but I can't claim for certain that our crew actually bombed Peenemunde at all. There was some sort of lock on the bomb-doors which the flight engineer was supposed to release beforehand. He forgot to do this. The bomb aimer announced over the intercom that the bomb-doors wouldn't open, and there followed a mad panic by the flight engineer to release the locking mechanism. We gave the bombs the push, but I wouldn't swear that we actually hit Peenemunde, although we can't have been very far out. Perhaps we ought to have gone round again, but to be honest, flying at five thousand feet among all that stuff was really sticking your neck out and we felt we'd done enough.

Perhaps it was just as well we didn't dawdle any longer, because immediately afterwards we were coned by searchlights. We were too low to dive, which would have been the normal evasive action, but Johnny at once began throwing the aircraft all over the sky – with no effect at all. The beams held us like glue. I believe the master searchlight that the Germans used to have – it had a blue beam – was controlled by radar, and the other lights were geared up to it, so once the blue one had you, you were hooked. Anyway there we were on the spit and ready for roasting, and it seemed an eternity – though in reality probably about five minutes – before they lost us. Yet all that time, believe it or not, the Germans didn't fire a single shot at us. The reason for our escape, in fact, was that there was another aircraft coned at the same time and the flak guns were all concentrating on him. By the time they'd finished shooting him down we were well out of range.

This was the nastiest raid we ever experienced, and altogether we did sweat a bit that night. We were very glad indeed to get back home. Even so, the aircraft wasn't damaged and neither were we. This was pretty lucky when you consider that half the aircraft that went from Middleton St George didn't even come back.

People have suggested to me since the war that seeing losses of this sort happening ought to have frightened me out of my wits. It is true that in the short time I was with the squadron I only knew of one crew that finished its tour of thirty operations. The empty chairs appeared night after night, just as in the war films, but whereas in the films there's always a great drama about this, with pretty WAAFs fighting back the tears and the Wingco Flying all tight-lipped, the truth is that, on our squadron at least, it didn't much bother anyone – certainly not the crews. Perhaps the losses themselves were responsible. The whole point is that my crew was scarcely on the squadron long enough to get to know anyone properly, and as a matter of fact I don't think many other people were either. Nobody lasted long enough. The disappearance of people whose names you could barely fit to their faces produced little impact. Our feelings were that the other crews were either already there when we arrived, so they didn't count, or else they joined us afterwards, so they didn't count either. Under these circumstances I find it difficult to say anything much about squadron spirit, morale and so on. To be frank, there just wasn't any: I never cared tuppence about the squadron as such, nor did the rest of our crew. But we did care about each other, and this extended to our ground crew as well. They looked after our aircraft alone, and our confidence in them was total. Nothing, absolutely nothing, was too much trouble, and they nursed our aircraft as though their lives depended on it as well as ours. We had a system whereby they took us out on the beer one week and we took them out the next. Since they were Canadians they could afford it better than we could, because their pay as ground crew was higher than ours as aircrew (except for Chris, of course). I particularly point this out, not because it rankled with us, but because I want to stress that it didn't. We were a happy group together, and if there was indeed on the squadron as a whole anything that could be described as high morale, it was within the individual crews that it was generated.

The crews from the other squadron on the station always went to Darlington and ours always went to Stockton: don't ask me why. We usually went out for a meal and then we would go on the beer. And at this point I must explode the commonly held fallacy about aircrew fitness. The truth is that you couldn't have found a bigger set of boozers anywhere in the three Services. Nobody in our crew made the slightest effort to keep fit: on the contrary, you'd have thought we were trying to kill ourselves with alcoholic poisoning. The same applied to all other aircrew I ever met. (I often wonder if it's the same today.)

Our weekly thrashes followed a set pattern. First we'd have a meal, nearly always at the same restaurant. They got used to us, and I've no doubt at all they put themselves out a lot for us, because in spite of the wartime shortages we always got a splendid meal, and the fact is it cost us very little. After that we'd go to the pictures, and then I'm sorry to say we'd make the rounds of all the pubs and get pie-eyed. How we ever managed to get back from Stockton I don't know. As a matter of fact there were some occasions when we didn't. And this was where the staff of the local bus station rescued us. It was well known to the servicemen of the district that if you'd missed your last bus or train, you could always get a kip-down for the night on a double-decker bus – and they'd wake you up next morning with a cup of tea and a bun in time for the first bus or train. These are the sort of kindnesses you met with in wartime, and you don't forget.

We were not billeted at Middleton St George but in a country house about half an hour's MT run away from the airfield. It was called Dinsdale Hall: naturally we christened it Doomsday Hall. It was all oak panelling, wide staircases and draughts. The officers lived on camp, of course, and I've often wondered whether they really used to relieve their feelings with schooner races, leapfrog and high cockalorum in the mess as the books of war memoirs say. Anyway the NCOs didn't: not on our squadron. We were either on ops, or we were boozing in Stockton. At Doomsday Hall we only slept it off. I believe a dance was once arranged, but an op was put on and so it was scrubbed.

We knew little and cared less about how the officers lived, not because we were anti-officers but because our paths were separate from theirs. We were no more interested in them than they were in us. Of course there were many mixed crews in Bomber Command, and I believe it was practically unheard-of for any friction to be caused by the differences in rank. But as it happened, our crew scarcely saw an officer except at briefings and debriefings.

TELEGRAM

Office Stamp: YORKSHIRE 6 OC 43

Prefix: 9
109 12.41 DL/T CHMS 57

PRIORITY CC MR FLEE 4 HIRSTWOOD RD SHIPLEY YORKS =

REGRET TO INFORM YOU THAT YOURSON SGT NORMAN LEE IS MISSING AS THE RESULT OF AIR OPERATIONS ON THE NIGHT OF 4TH OCT 1943 LETTER FOLLOWS ANY FURTHER INFORMATION RECEIVED WILL BE IMMEDIATELY COMMUNICATED TO YOU XY THE AIR MINISTRY = CC UNIT +

IV

Shot Down

When we were told at briefing on 23 August 1943, "You're going to the Big City tonight," a great cheer went round the whole room; there was not a shadow of doubt that everybody was looking forward to bombing Berlin. A ring was drawn round a sector of the city on the briefing map. The briefing officer pointed to it and said, "This is where you bomb, and the next time you hit Berlin you'll bomb the area adjacent to it, and so on until the city is completely flattened."

This was the policy as far as Berlin was concerned. We knew it perfectly well, though I am not sure that the general public quite understood it at the time. We knew we were being sent to bomb civilians. I can't answer for all the other aircrews, but as far as ours was concerned it didn't bother us. We felt that the Germans had only themselves to blame. They had started it, and now we were finishing it.

Berlin apart, it was military targets that Bomber Command operations as a whole were aimed at, though we understood very well that the 'area bombing' concept inevitably included a lot of civilians getting killed. Our view was that the general objective was a military one, and if civilians happened to be in the way, it was just too bad.

I suppose we were able to feel this way because there was no personal contact. It wasn't like a couple of infantrymen slugging it out with bayonets. It was just a technical job, delivering the bombs to the place they were supposed to be delivered to, letting them go and then returning home again. We didn't think about the people we were killing because we didn't see them.

Although I've pondered about it a good deal since those days, it would be hypocritical to say I've ever lost any sleep, and I think the man who pushes the nuclear button will react no differently. If he has any thoughts he will just be hoping that the thing he lets off will wipe out the opposition sufficiently thoroughly to prevent them from retaliating in kind. And he'll think about his own family and hope they'll be all right. Where we were killing tens and hundreds, he'll be killing hundreds of thousands, but it will mean no more to him than it did to us, again because there'll be no personal contact.

It was quite a different matter later on in France when I was with the Maquis. Seeing the people you're shooting at makes you dry in the mouth, especially when you hit them; and hearing the bullets whistling round your unprotected body is quite another thing from seeing flak from the inside of an aeroplane. No noise at all penetrated the aircraft from outside, because the sound of the engines drowned everything. To us the whole affair was just a silent firework display, like Cinerama with the sound turned off. The searchlights poked about the sky. The flak bursts made puffballs all around. The town below quietly burned and exploded. We were no more than spectators of it all. The only sense of reality came from the smell of cordite produced by the flak; this used to come through despite the oxygen masks.

If this gives the impression that I wasn't very frightened on any of my operations you'd be about right, and I think that went for the rest of our crew too. But you must remember that until the night we were shot down we'd never been hit or hurt in any way, despite our few brushes with searchlights and fighters. We sometimes heard the faint rattling of shrapnel on the fuselage, but nothing that did any damage.

Berlin turned out to be no different from the other cities we bombed except as a symbol. Although ours was, I believe, the first really heavy attack on the capital, the raid was just routine – at least so far as our crew was concerned, which was all that mattered. There was a lot of flak on the approaches, as might be expected, but over the city itself there was no trouble at all. As a kind of special treat for Hitler's capital we took along, in addition to our official bomb-load, a couple of bricks and two empty beer-bottles with bent razor-blades inserted in the neck. Empty bottles treated like this whistle just like real bombs going down.

This was our eighth operation, so by now we were really old hands. We went on leave on 24 August for seven days, returning to the squadron about the end of the month. As far as I can recall, aircrew on operations were entitled to leave every six weeks or thereabouts. Lord Nuffield used to pay five shillings a day special allowance to every member of aircrew when on leave. This was a lot of money in those days, and it must have cost him a fortune. In many cases the brewers probably had good reason to thank the noble lord for his generosity, though not in mine. Facing the flak and night-fighters while sober was one thing: to face my parents while drunk would have been something else again.

The only time I saw a man go to pieces was on our return from leave. There was an air gunner on the squadron who joined our train at York. He ought to have returned the day before, but had some compassionate reason for not having done so. When we got back to Middleton St George he learned that his crew had returned on time, gone on ops that night and gone missing. He had a complete nervous collapse and had to be taken off flying immediately.

I never knew of anyone else being taken off operations. People often seem to have the impression that you could get off ops any time by just refusing to go. This was not really quite the case. It was true that you could see the MO and tell him you didn't feel well. He'd take you off for a limited period, but that was all.

Of course, if you insisted that you just weren't going to fly any more, full stop, no one would actually push you into the aircraft and strap you down, because obviously a passenger as unwilling as that would be a menace to everyone else on board. You would be stripped of your tapes for 'LMF' (lack of moral fibre), so if you really wanted out this was the only exit. I did hear of one or two individuals who did it. I believe what happened was that they were remustered to some sort of menial trade or even thrown out, which meant being called up for the Army right away. Even if I'd been tempted to throw my hand in, this latter would have been sufficient deterrent, because to me the Army always looked like a fate worse than death and still does.

Our first noteworthy operation after leave was on 15th September, when we bombed the Modane Tunnel on the Italian side of the Alps. There was a railway marshalling yard situated right between the mountains, and for once the spectacle appealed even to my stolid imagination. The incendiaries made an interesting show as they dropped, because a lot of them hit the sides of mountains and bounced down into the valley. The walls of the valley reflected the glow of the fires and the flashes of the explosions, so that even though we were at eighteen thousand feet or so we could see the outlines of the buildings quite plainly.

There were no searchlights and no flak, just as on the Milan trip. I don't know if all the Italian targets were defenceless, but the two we attacked certainly seemed to be.

This raid was followed by two totally uneventful trips to 'Happy Valley' (the Ruhr industrial belt). Then, on the night of 22 September, we went to Mannheim. On this night the Germans did something I'd never seen before. About a quarter of an hour's flying time before we reached the target they had laid a trail of flares all the way in. It was just like flying down a well-lit main road. The fighters attacked from the dark part of the sky. We ourselves were very lucky as usual: no one had a go at us. There can be little doubt, however, that the Germans had had some kind of forewarning of what the target was that night: in plain language, there must have been a breach of security to enable them to prepare our reception in this way.

This was also the first time we had put our own fighters over the target area. They were Mosquitoes, I believe, and it felt quite odd, but very comforting, to see them there.

When we were crossing the Channel on the way home our starboard inner engine developed an oil leak and my rear turret mechanism became unserviceable, so we put out a Mayday call. This was just an excuse really: we wanted to make a diversion landing in Sussex so that Johnny could visit his girlfriend, who was stationed somewhere there. Anyway they brought us in at Ford, and while we were waiting to land there was a Lancaster also in the circuit and in a much worse state than we were. He had an engine on fire, and the pilot kept repeating over the R/T, "This is Q for Queenie, this is Q for Queenie, this is Q for Queenie," over and over again, in a rather posh BBC-type accent. His Aussie mid-upper gunner got fed up with this and interrupted him, shouting out, "Oh fer Chrarssike, bagger Q fer Queenie, let's jast get bladdy well in!"

He did get in all right, and so did we. After landing we stopped outside Air Traffic Control and opened our bomb-doors with a fire-tender standing by. This was normal procedure in case of 'hang-ups' (bombs that had failed to leave the bomb-bay when the button was pressed over the target). On this occasion, as it happened, a shower of incendiaries fell out and burst into flames, but the fire-tender had them out in seconds, so there was no trouble.

The Wingco Flying was out meeting the crews, because he was particularly anxious to hear whether we'd seen any of our Mosquito fighters over the target area. The young pilot officer from Q for Queenie kept pushing himself forward in front of Johnny, who was only a flight-sergeant. He didn't half burble on, and he rather gave the impression of having flown on dozens of operations. The 35 bomb-symbols painted on the fuselage of his Lanc seemed to bear this out – until it finally transpired from his answers to the Wingco's questioning that he'd only just taken over the aircraft and that in fact this had been his first operational trip. When the Wingco realised this, he fairly blew a gasket, telling the pilot officer to wait his turn and let someone with experience speak, "Like the flight-sergeant here, for instance".

Poor lad, his excitement was probably just the result of nervous reaction after his adventures. There's no doubt we all felt a bit that way after an op – even individuals like me with no imagination and crews like ours which never got hit or ran into trouble.

This probably accounts for the talkativeness of crews in the circuit waiting to land. With about thirty aircraft to bring in at Middleton, for instance, landing took some time. Air Traffic Control gave each aircraft a number as it reported in. Then they stacked you at five-hundred foot intervals, gradually moving you down from level to level in the circuit until eventually your turn came to land. It was a pretty impatient business while you were waiting, and I must admit that we were pretty free with our language as we chatted. It even surprised me to discover just how free it was when we were taken into the briefing room one morning and they played back a tape they had made of the conversation that had come over the R/T the night before. It was embarrassing to find that the identities of the individual speakers came across so distinctly.

It was possible for local people to pick up these conversations on their wireless sets, and believe it or not there were the odd one or two who would write letters or phone the station with complaints about things they'd heard. There was a complaint about our crew one night. I think Johnny had urged ATC to pull their fingers out or something like that, and of course this was a good many years before the Duke of Edinburgh made that particular expression respectable! I must say I did rather feel that people had no bloody business listening in if they were so sensitive.

Their attitude was quite a contrast to that of the WAAF MT driver who sort of 'adopted' our crew. She always made a point of coming out to our dispersal point to meet us. She was a sweet girl and a complete lady and despite the fact that our conversation and language were often filthy when we got out of the aircraft, she never turned a hair.

Then there was the old C of E padre, who used to cycle round the aircraft at takeoff with water-bottles slung round him in case anyone was feeling thirsty before setting off. The middle bottle always had whisky in it. Goodness knows where he got it from in wartime, and of course it was quite against regulations. For my own part, I never had a 'nip', but it was always there if anyone did feel like it. I don't know whether the old boy was any good as a preacher, but in my opinion he was an expert on Christian charity!

Any former member of a Bomber Command aircrew will recall some episode similar to the following one, which happened one night when we were all in the circuit over Middleton St George. We were all waiting to come down when one pilot chipped in and said, "Request priority to land: am on two engines."

Of course they gave him priority and he got down before everyone else. It was quite true as well, he was indeed on two engines, because he was flying a Wellington, which only had two engines to start with! The Halifax crews didn't think this was at all funny of course – until afterwards.

On another occasion a German intruder got in among the returning aircraft and shot one of them up. All he managed to do was wound the rear gunner slightly. The Germans used to beat up our bombers over the base airfields in this way quite often, I believe, but this was the only time I had personal knowledge of its happening.

When you go to see films about the war, there are always dramatic sequences in which aircraft come back with a couple of engines on fire, the fuselage full of holes and half the crew bleeding to death from ghastly injuries. I have no doubt that this used to happen sometimes, but I wonder if these 'wing-and-a-prayer' incidents were as common as the films suggest? My own operational life lasted only a matter of ten weeks, but things moved fast in those days and although I certainly knew of plenty of aircraft that never came back at all, I witnessed only one occasion when a Halifax came back with wounded aboard.

Our crew certainly never reckoned on anything of this sort as much of a probability: we might have been less carefree if we had. Our assumption was that if your aircraft was hit, there was very little chance of getting out. You'd drop like a stone, fall completely out of the sky and never know anything about the finish because you'd be unconscious.

Insofar as we thought about it at all, which wasn't much or often, we expected a quick death and a clean one. If anything did worry us it was the idea of being hit by flak or a fighter on the way to the target and the bombs going off. We certainly felt happier coming out than going in. When the bombs went, the whole aircraft used to lift, and so did our spirits. Yet when you think of it, this was not very logical, because if a quick death was what we wanted, getting blown up by our own bombs would certainly have done the trick. Nevertheless, we always believed that for most people, when you were hit that was the finish: you just didn't come back. This, in our opinion, was why those who did come back had very little of note to report: this one had been coned by searchlights for a minute or two, that one had dodged a fighter or got a couple of flak-holes in the tailplane, but never anything startling. I don't say the dramatic stuff in the books written by war heroes didn't happen: of course it did, I only say it didn't happen often, and never to anyone I knew – which seems reasonable enough when you think about it, otherwise we'd all have got the VC. Most people either came back in one piece or not at all.

At any rate, our crew's time had not yet come, and our next trip, to Bochum on a twenty-minute thousand-bomber 'saturation' raid, was entirely without incident as far as we were concerned. We saw nothing except the customary fireworks, did nothing except drop our bombs on the target, and flew home again to bacon and eggs and a nice warm bed. This trip typified what aircrew meant when they called an op "a piece of piss" (usually translated as "a piece of cake" for civilian consumption). It wasn't high spirits or bravado that made us say this; it was a precise description of just how easy it could be.

After the Bochum raid Johnny, our pilot, was called in by the flight commander and told that our crew had done enough for the time being; we hadn't missed a trip except when we were on leave and it was time we were stood down for a rest. Furthermore, he said, he wasn't sending us out again until after our next leave, which would soon be due. On the night of the next op, whatever it was, we stayed behind. But we went out to the airfield and watched them take off. It felt most peculiar, seeing the big silhouettes of the aircraft against the night sky, hearing the engines revving, watching the old padre scooting round on his bike with his customary cargo of illegal whisky and legal wakey-wakey tablets, knowing that tonight it was nothing to do with us. It was a strange mixture of relief and uneasiness, like smoking in the playground at the end of your last day at school. I can't say we liked it much.

We liked it even less the following day, because the newly-arrived crew who had taken our aircraft on that trip didn't bring it back. Crews liked to keep their own aircraft, and we were no exceptions. We had become attached to S for Sugar, and I'm afraid we felt more indignation at the crew for losing her than sympathy with them for getting shot down on their first time out! We might not have minded so much if we had gone on leave on 5th October according to plan. However, on the morning of the 4th, our Flight Commander again sent for Johnny and told him that tonight's target was a bad one and that although he had promised not to send us on any more trips until after our leave, he wanted only experienced crews out that night. With all the operations we'd done, we most emphatically fell into that category, so we were detailed after all.

None of us was pleased at the news, especially when we learned that the target was Frankfurt. Chris, the mid-upper gunner, was particularly sceptical about it and kept saying that we ought not to be going so deep into Germany. Whether he was having a premonition I wouldn't like to say, but he certainly wasn't happy about the trip.

We weren't exactly thrilled to bits with our new aeroplane either. Although there was nothing wrong with it – indeed, it was supposed to be better, being a later mark than our old one – it had a mid-upper turret, which we were not keen on because we'd never had one before. We much preferred to have Chris on the floor searching below the aircraft for fighters. In view of what happened that night it would appear that our misgivings were justified.

We took off from Middleton St George for our seventeenth and – as it turned out – last operation at 1725 hours on 4th October 1943. As far as I can recall it would have been about a nine-hour run to Frankfurt and back if we had completed the journey. The weather was clear, with a good moon, and although we called this "Bomber Harris's moon" it was not our cup of tea. Our personal choice was for plenty of cloud to make things difficult for night-fighters and to give us somewhere to hide if one happened to spot us. On this trip there was to be a navigation aid that we'd never used before. An aircraft of the Pathfinder Force would lay a marker on track to assist following aircraft. I believe the idea of it was to help cut out the confusion and collisions over the target caused by aircraft coming in from different directions.

We were about thirty minutes flying time short of Frankfurt, on our way in, when we passed over the marker, so it must have been about ten to nine in the evening. This was when we were attacked by fighters. No doubt they realised that the marker was some sort of navigation aid and had used it themselves to locate us.

The first thing I saw was a Junkers 88 about three hundred feet astern of us, slightly to starboard and climbing. I immediately told Johnny, using the standard reporting procedure.

"Rear gunner to pilot – prepare to corkscrew starboard – corkscrew starboard down. Go!"

The drill was to fall away to starboard in the direction of the attacking fighter, then roll and climb, and keep on repeating this sequence until you threw him off.

Johnny promptly flung the aircraft into this manoeuvre – successfully, I think, because as far as I could tell the Junkers I had spotted never fired his guns. But there must have been another fighter working with him...

We were well into the starboard turn and were beginning to fall away when we were raked from underneath by the second fighter. He did a first-class job on our starboard wing, because the engines on that side burst instantly into two huge balls of flame.

I saw the starboard aileron sail past the tail and disappear. As it went, the flames from the engines were shooting past my rear turret on the starboard side. I remember Scotty, the flight engineer, yelling over the intercom, "The whole bloody aircraft's on fire!"

Indeed it was. The flames had reached back down the petrol feed-lines and were setting the inside of the fuselage ablaze. Nobody seemed to have been hit. [In fact Scotty had been wounded in the left arm. I found this out when I got back to England, because Scotty had already been repatriated from Germany. This used to be done with some of the wounded. At the hospital in England they told him the German surgeons had done a marvellous job in saving his arm.]

There was no panic whatsoever, since there wasn't time for that to develop, and it was all over in a few seconds. I remember Johnny calling over the intercom, "This is it, lads, get the hell out of it!"

I didn't need to be told twice, and I don't think anyone else paused to say goodbye either, because it was very easy to see no one had any future staying in the aircraft. I centralised the turret, opened the turret doors and grabbed my parachute, which was hanging inside the fuselage. Having clipped the chute on, I swung the turret round to point the guns to starboard so as to bale out on the port side away from the flames. I got my fingers above the door, climbed up on the seat and let go. The correct drill was to roll out backwards, but I didn't fancy this, so I went feet first. You were supposed to count ten before pulling the ripcord, but I think I just shouted "One-two-three-ten!" and heaved.

No one had ever warned me to keep my head back after pulling the ripcord – perhaps it wouldn't have been necessary if I'd rolled out backwards as I'd been told – so I was quite surprised when the pilot chute shot past my nose. The main chute came next with a hell of a whip, followed by a thump, then an upward jerk on my chest and shoulders and there I was... dangling by my armpits on a cold night, 18 thousand feet up somewhere over Europe, wondering what part I was going to play in the war next.

If anyone had told me, I'd have been extremely surprised...

Forged identity document, describing Norman Lee as a deaf-mute Frenchman.

V

Evasion

I'd never jumped before (for that matter, I've never done it since and don't want to either!). The only practice we had ever had was at air gunnery school where they had a harness suspended from the roof of the hangar. We used to fasten ourselves into this and jump off a pair of steps onto a mat, to simulate a parachute landing. Just before hitting the ground you unclipped the quick-release and rolled on the mat. They taught us how to absorb the impact, by rolling over onto the right shoulder. This is very easy in daylight, but it was night when I landed for real and there was a ground mist as well, which made it a much more difficult proposition.

There was a fairish wind blowing as I floated down, and I could tell I was drifting quite a bit. They say that by working your shrouds and lines and things you can control your fall, and I dare say you can, but when I experimented I had no success at all. In any case there didn't seem to be much point in it, since I couldn't make out anything on the ground, so I soon gave up. As long as I was going down safely, I was quite happy. My only worry was that I could hear the engines of all the other aircraft heading for Frankfurt and I kept thinking to myself, "If some aeroplane comes along up here, am I going to find myself dangling underneath it like a worm on a fishing-line?"

Of course nothing like that happened, and as the seconds ticked by, the aircraft noise receded and I began to think about my landing. I remembered that you are supposed to relax to take the fall, and I got myself into the proper posture when I judged my altitude to be about fifteen hundred feet. But then I plunged into a heavy ground mist and lost all sense of height, so when I struck the ground I did so unexpectedly. Nevertheless, being in the relaxed posture, I didn't do myself any real damage, though it wasn't a textbook landing by any means. I landed on my toes in the approved manner and started the roll, but I never completed it. Since I had been unable to see anything I couldn't release my harness just before touching down as you are supposed to, so I was dragged by the parachute and at once discovered what is meant by 'seeing stars'. I hit the side of my face on what I thought must be a concrete runway or something. In fact, it was a ploughed field and I was lucky it was October or the earth might have been a lot harder.

I managed to get free of the parachute after recovering from the shock of landing, and stood up and looked around. The field in which I had landed was on a hillside and surrounded by trees. Everything was quiet and I was 'in one piece'. I didn't want to have to give myself up, besides, there was nobody about to give myself up to. There was also no visible means of transport available. I was going to have to walk home...

It was only when I actually did get home many months later, that I heard what had happened to the rest of the crew. Except for Chris, the mid-upper gunner, they were all supposed to go out of the front escape hatch. This was jammed, however, probably because of the aircraft being shot up, so the whole crew had to come back to the rear entrance hatch, where we used to get into the aircraft at takeoff. Johnny stayed at the controls until they had all jumped, and for some reason believed that I was still in the turret because – according to his recollection – I was still talking to him over the intercom and he kept telling me to bale out. For my own part, I don't for a moment believe this was so, because frankly, with the possible exception of the bomb aimer, who was standing at the hatch releasing 'window' at the time the fighter shot us up, I don't think anyone beat me out of that aircraft! However, this was Johnny's impression. When he finally left the controls and came to the rear hatch, he saw the turret swinging and nobody in it, so he concluded I had gone. He then baled out himself.

Johnny walked into Belgium after parachuting, made contact with the underground and ten weeks later was back in England. During his interrogation at the Air Ministry he was told that the Germans had notified through the Swiss Red Cross that a body had been found in the aircraft wreckage. He naturally decided in view of his earlier doubts that this must have been me, and when he reported all this to the interrogating officer a telegram was duly sent to my family altering my status from 'missing' to 'believed killed'. Hence, for almost a year my family at home thought I was dead.

Chris, the mid-upper gunner, joined me later in Luxembourg. Don Richards, the navigator, was picked up the following morning by the Germans, and so was Scotty, the flight engineer, who had lost a lot of blood from his wound and was in quite a bad way. Alec Parkinson, the wireless operator, landed very near a village, which seems to have been in Luxembourg because the Germans were conducting a house-to-house search with the Gestapo in attendance, and he ran slap into them.

Stan Baldwin, the bomb aimer, landed safely and apparently in high spirits, as usual. It was typical of Stan that he decided to hitchhike home. He put up his thumb to the first vehicle that he saw. It stopped, and the two German officers travelling in it invited him to join them. That was the end of Stan's bid for freedom!

The four who were taken prisoner all met up again when they were put in the local jail. They were moved by train to Frankfurt a day or so later. The interrogation centre for all captured aircrew was located just outside Frankfurt – which was the city we had been bombing the night we were shot down. Since this was only a day or so later, perhaps it's not surprising that there was an ugly scene on Frankfurt station when a mob of civilians gathered round and wanted to lynch the prisoners. But even this didn't subdue Stan Baldwin the irrepressible. I understand that he entertained the German guards during the journey by putting a black comb over his upper lip and giving an impersonation of Hitler. Apparently the guards found this very amusing, although his fellow prisoners didn't. They were terrified and told him for God's sake to pack it in. I don't blame them, but Stan's tactlessness was quite typical: nothing ever worried him.

Of course I knew nothing of all this at the time. I was not even sure which country I was in, because 30 minutes' flying time short of Frankfurt it was a toss-up whether I was in Germany or Luxembourg. I couldn't even be sure what time it was – though I figured it must be around nine o'clock – because my watch had been U/S so I had left it behind at Middleton. The aircraft would have veered off course quite a bit in the few seconds before we baled out, then I suppose it took about 20 minutes to come down by

Irrepressible bomb aimer 'Stan' Baldwin, who, having been captured, entertained his German guards with impressions of Adolf Hitler.

parachute because I had jumped at about 17 or 18 thousand feet. With a strong wind blowing, I knew I would have drifted a good way, but I didn't have any idea in which direction, of course, because I never bothered to remember what drift we had when we were flying, even though I used to help the navigator determine it from time to time.

I took my parachute, flying kit, rank chevrons and brevet into the woods and buried them under a heap of dead leaves. I seemed to have discarded my helmet on the way down; anyhow I was no longer wearing it. The biggest problem was my flying boots. I believe that about this time they were bringing in what were called 'escape boots', the tops of which you could cut off so they resembled civilian footwear, but the ones I had were the big suede type, which were very difficult to hide. I managed to tuck them under my trousers, but they were very conspicuous just the same.

One item I did have was a pocket compass sewn into the lining of my battledress blouse, so I wasn't completely helpless. Of course we had been instructed that if we had to bale out we weren't to give ourselves up but to contact the nearest underground group or make for Spain, or both. I had no idea how to find an underground group, but I did know that Spain lay roughly southwest, so I began walking in that direction. The countryside was very hilly, and I walked through fields for what I thought was a couple of hours without ever crossing a road. At one point I crossed a barbed-wire fence, which I felt fairly certain was the frontier between Germany and Luxembourg. There were no border patrols between the two countries, because Hitler had declared that Luxembourg was a part of Germany. He annexed it, changed all the street-names to German ones and abolished the frontier barriers, insisting that there was no difference between Luxembourg and Germany. Fortunately the Luxembourgers didn't agree with him, and that's how I was able to avoid ending up in a German POW camp...

I was in my normal state of aircrew unfitness, and I found this plodding over rough country exhausting work after a day that had already been quite active, so I settled under some bushes for a kip. It wasn't very comfortable and I kept dozing off and waking by turns. All I had on was my battledress, so it was rather chilly in the early hours of the morning. I finally shook myself into life about dawn, remembered my 'escape kit' and began exploring it.

Believe it or not, we had never been briefed on how to use this kit, we just drew it each time we went on an op and handed it in again when we got back. No one had ever told us what it consisted of and we had never enquired either – aircrew were always optimists – so there were faults on both sides. I met many shot-down fliers later on and never found anyone who had been better briefed on escaping than I had or who had known beforehand what the escape kit contained. (By contrast, all the aircrew escapers in books and films seem to be thoroughly clued-up about what to do; I sometimes wonder if we were in the same Air Force!)

I emptied the escape pack, sorted the stuff out and tried to figure what it was all for. There were some Horlicks tablets, which I ate, and a bar of chocolate green with mould. I didn't bother with that, but ate instead another bar that I had been carrying in a pocket of my battledress. I washed this lot down with the tin of flying-ration orange juice from the night before. (Amazingly, after I landed I had found this stuffed down the front of my battledress blouse!) There was a rubber bag which I afterwards realised was for carrying water; at the time I thought it was some kind of tobacco pouch. Some water-purifying tablets went with this. Then there was a tube containing a whitish liquid, which turned out to be condensed milk. (One Canadian I met later in France told me that when he found the tube of condensed milk he didn't know what it was, but he used it for sore feet and it was very good! Someone else I met thought it was toothpaste.)

That was all there was in the food line, but there were some other items too. There was a little money – Belgian and French francs equivalent to about thirty shillings, which I suppose would be worth something like thirty or forty pounds today. They were careful not to trust us with too much! A pocket compass and a map of Europe printed on a silk handkerchief square, showing most of Germany, Luxembourg, Belgium, Holland, France and the Spanish frontier, completed the outfit. It looked fairly encouraging, so I repacked it all and set off walking again, keeping to the hills and woods as far as I could and continuing to head in a general south-westerly direction.

The countryside was still pretty open, and although I did cross a few roads they were just country lanes. The fields, hedges and trees were peppered with bits of 'window' dropped by our aircraft the night before. I learned from the local people later on that they thought it was some kind of incendiary device and were afraid it might burst into flames and destroy the crops, so they used to go round carefully collecting every single piece they could find, which must have been a monumental task. At one point I saw an orchard as I emerged from a wood. There were some apples and pears still on the trees, and I was approaching with the idea of helping myself when I saw someone moving. This was the only person I had seen all day. I doubled back at once and kept to the woods from then on. It was a very nice day, bright and sunny and quite pleasant for walking, but by about three in the afternoon I was getting rather tired and hungry. It was about then that I found myself approaching a road-bridge across a river. It was fairly busy with pedestrians, cyclists and farm carts. If I wanted to continue south-westward I was going to have to cross the river too. On the bridge there were German troops, however, and they were holding up the traffic and searching people and vehicles.

I hesitated for a while, watching from the shelter of the trees and trying to decide what to do. I came to the conclusion that I would have to hide up until night, then try to swim the river during darkness. I retreated among the trees again and ran slap into an old peasant woman.

I don't know which of us was more surprised. We stood and stared at one another for a few seconds without speaking. Then she smiled and pointed at me and said, "You Engländer?"

Considering the sort of clothes I was wearing I could scarcely deny it, and anyway it didn't take much doing to guess that she was friendly, so I said, "Yes."

That was it. She flung her arms round me and kissed me on both cheeks. When I managed to come up for air she asked me if I had helped to bomb Frankfurt the night before. When I said I had, she was as pleased as Punch and we had another love scene. It was clear I had nothing to worry about from her. I managed to make out quite a lot of what she said, perhaps from the smattering of German and French I had learnt at school, and it's surprising what you can do with a bit of sign-language and a lot of goodwill.

The lady's husband was ploughing up in the fields, and she was just taking him his tea. He never got it because she gave it to me, and short work I made of it, because I hadn't eaten anything since being shot down except for my rather sparse impromptu breakfast. Meanwhile the old lady went off to fetch her husband, and although I was just finishing off the last of his grub by the time he arrived, he was very pleased to see me. I found another bar of Cadbury's Dairy Milk in my battledress, and since he hadn't seen anything like it for years, he regarded it as a fair exchange for his sandwiches. He couldn't stop slapping me on the back in his glee. Eventually he took me back into the woods and showed me a place to hide. He left me for about an hour, then returned with some bread, part of a cooked chicken and a bottle of wine. He told me to stay where I was until dark, when he would bring someone to collect me and take me into the village. I tucked into the food and wine: in fact, I was so thirsty that I fairly flung the wine down. By the time I realised it was heavily fortified with cognac it was too late, so that when the old boy came back with two other men to pick me up at about eight or nine o'clock I was, quite honestly, as tight as a tick. They dressed me in a trilby hat and a long raincoat down to my ankles while I grinned and giggled. I don't think I can have looked much of a credit to the Air Force as I was escorted staggering into the village dressed in this strange outfit!

They took me to a house in the village where I was to stay. When inside, I found to my astonishment that half the population of the village appeared to be crowded into it, waiting to greet me. They were jabbering away excitedly and clumping about the place making a terrible racket, but this didn't stop them telling me to keep my voice down because there was a curfew and the Germans were patrolling the streets. In fact, I scarcely said a word the whole evening but just sat watching the performance and recovering from my encounter with the fortified wine. The party didn't break up until about two in the morning, by which time I was fairly whacked.

The people of the house – husband, wife and two sons aged fifteen and seventeen – had fixed me up with a bedroom, and I stayed with them for the best part of three weeks. It was a pleasant little house, but I never knew very much about where it was located or what the village looked like, because I never went outside until I left. In any case, it had always been impressed on us during training that for security reasons we must avoid finding out where we were or the identities of people helping us to escape.

When I was stationed in Germany after the war I tried to discover where I had been. As far as I could make out it was a small frontier village called Dillingen, and if that was so I must have entered it from the German side, because the bridge I had to cross was the frontier post. In that case

I had been wrong in my impression that I crossed the frontier while walking over the fields on the night we were shot down. The family I stayed with must have been a Luxembourg family living slightly on the German side of the border. The man of the house was the head of the local underground and he and his two sons – or so I heard after the war – were ultimately detected by the Germans and executed.

One day while in Dillingen I was delighted to hear that Chris, our mid-upper gunner, was safe and well, having been picked up by the underground, and was being looked after by two old spinsters in a house not far away. The lady of my house visited the two old dears one day and brought me a brief note from Chris, in which the most startling item of news was that he was made to take a nap every afternoon to "keep up his strength and aid his digestion."

As to my own digestion, it was working overtime. There was a fresh supply of cigars and cognac every day. The food was marvellous, and I can only think that the villagers were sending it in from hoarded stocks, because the two sons of the household said they hadn't eaten like this since the war started.

As a matter of fact, the same applied to me. I was so well fed that there was one mealtime when I just couldn't face anything: my stomach needed a rest. I didn't know how to explain this properly, but by saying *"Nein"* and patting my stomach I seemed to get the message across, because they didn't give me anything. The next day, however, I happened to receive another note from Chris, which puzzled me by expressing his sympathy for my stomach ailment and his hope that the doctor would be able to fix me up. The doctor duly turned up. He spoke English well, and began by saying that he was sorry to hear about my upset stomach. I replied that there was nothing wrong with it except over-eating, and explained how the misunderstanding had arisen. We had a good laugh about it, and he gave me instructions how to deal with the situation if I had the same trouble again: the right way to tell them I was full up was to draw my hand across my throat in a cutting gesture! It was a great relief to be able to have a chat in my own language after the days of pidgin-English. The doctor stayed quite some time and left me a number of English paperbacks, which were a blessing.

Bit by bit my civilian clothing was gathered together – not an easy matter in wartime, but the biggest hold-up was getting me an identity card. Eventually they got over this, however, and a photographer came and took my picture. At last I was ready, and they warned me I would be moving shortly.

Then one evening they brought Chris over. It was certainly grand to see one another again, but I couldn't congratulate him on his appearance. The trouble was he was six foot two, blonde like a German, and very difficult to clothe. His trouser bottoms were about three or four inches above his ankles, while the jacket of his suit was big enough for me to have got into it with him. However, his overcoat was a reasonable enough fit and covered his sins. I flatter myself that my own appearance was rather smarter, with a white shirt, a dark brown suit of excellent fit that I would gladly have gone for a job interview in, and a raincoat.

There was little time for chatting with Chris or expressing proper gratitude to the family who had sheltered me. A young man whom I hadn't seen before turned up as our guide. There were bicycles for us, and he was anxious to get moving. He warned us that we were going to cross the bridge and that when we came to it we must go like hell. I imagine that our departure was timed for some brief period when the German guards were not in attendance.

There were no lights on the bikes. It was a dark night and rather chilly, but it didn't take long to warm up, because our guide set a cracking pace and never paused or looked behind him. We took the bridge like competitors in the Tour de France, but there was no sign of trouble. Chris and I were soon jiggered and we slackened off at the other side, but it was obvious at once that our guide had no intention of doing likewise, and we had to redouble our efforts. In fact it was a nightmare of a ride, with little conversation but a lot of sweat and hard breathing, and I thought it would never end. I lost count of time, but eventually we reached the town of Medernach. Our guide delivered us to one of those bar-cum-restaurant-cum-guesthouse places that they have on the Continent, then disappeared quickly into the night. The lady of the house was big and jolly, and she greeted us with a big smile.

"Hello boys," she said. "Nice to see you. Everything fine here and you enjoy yourselves. My uncle is chef in London at the Savoy Hotel. You know it? When you get home, you go to see him, yes?"

This conversation set the tone of our stay there, and we thoroughly enjoyed the week we spent in the house. This was partly because we had a couple of escaping French POWs sharing the upstairs accommodation with us and partly because we ate so well.

The bar and restaurant were patronised a good deal by German soldiers, of course, but this never bothered us. The people of the house always warned us in good time, and all we had to do was keep quiet until the soldiers left. But it made us think a bit about the position of the people who were helping us. If we had been captured by the Germans, we would have been protected by the Geneva Convention as long as we had our identity discs and were unarmed. Ordinary German servicemen would respect this code without a doubt, and even the Gestapo would need a good excuse not to, but civilians caught giving us shelter would certainly have been shot.

Actually this bar-restaurant seemed to be a bit of a meeting-place for the local underground as well as for off-duty German soldiery. There were always odd characters popping in and out, and one day I was called into the kitchen to meet a couple of these chaps. They greeted me effusively – and showed me a battered-looking machine-gun which they wanted me to examine to see if it was serviceable. They said they had got it from the wreckage of an aircraft. I couldn't positively identify it as my own, of course, but it was certainly the correct type. However, it was minus its back-plate and therefore quite useless. It also had a bullet up the spout and could have gone off at any time, and the way they were handling it, it's a wonder it didn't!

We had been at the bar-restaurant for about a week when word reached the underground that the Gestapo were on our trail and we would have to be moved double-quick. We were sorry to leave. I had a silk scarf that I always used to wear as a lucky charm when flying, and I gave it to the lady of the house when we said goodbye. Chris and I said yes, we'd look up her uncle at the Savoy Hotel, and yes, we'd come back to visit after the war, but as it turned out we never did either of these things. I didn't have the nerve to walk into the Savoy Hotel, and I didn't know the uncle's name because we wouldn't let her tell us in case we were captured by the Germans and interrogated. After the war, when I was stationed in Germany, I went to Luxembourg to find the places I had passed through, but there were very few I could identify because, as I have said, we had deliberately avoided finding out where we were or the names of the people who helped us. I am not even sure that Medernach was the town where the bar-restaurant was situated.

We were moved to a largish detached house only a few hundred yards from the bar-restaurant but well isolated in a sheltered gully. The couple who owned it were oldish and obviously well-to-do – just the sort of people you would expect to be more concerned with enjoying their declining years peacefully than to risk their necks sheltering wanted men from the authorities. It just goes to show how strong the urge for freedom was in the occupied countries.

We only stayed one night in this house. The following evening two young girls, no more than eighteen or twenty years old, arrived to act as our escorts. We were warned not to speak to them at all but to follow a short distance behind them, so that if we were picked up they wouldn't be involved and could simply disappear.

The railway line passed right by the bar-restaurant, and the station, which was just a small concrete platform at one side of the single-line track, was practically adjacent. There was nobody about as we waited on the platform. The girls had bought our tickets for us from the bar-restaurant, but after that we carried out our instructions to the letter and gave no sign that we had anything to do with them. On the train we sat on the opposite side of the centre aisle to the girls, to all outward appearances ignoring them.

Our first train took us to the city of Luxembourg, where we followed the girls and changed to another train without having to pass through the barrier. This second train was very crowded, and lousy with German soldiers, two of whom got up and offered their seats to the girls. The occupation forces were under instructions at this period of the war to be on their best behaviour so as to create a good impression in the occupied countries – but we could very well have done without this piece of politeness, because the result of it was that Chris found himself standing next to one of these chaps. We stood in uncomfortable silence for ten minutes or so after pulling out of the station, then Chris horrified me by digging me in the ribs and whispering hoarsely, "The cord of my identity discs has broken and they've fallen on the floor. What shall I do?"

There they were, sure enough, looking as big as soup-plates.

"Well for crying out loud," I hissed, "pick them up and put them in your pocket. What else can you do?"

We needn't have worried, because the soldier was paying no attention to us whatsoever, and it wasn't long before we all got out at another station, where the girls led us straight to yet another train, which was practically empty. This third train took us to Differdange, a small town very close to the frontier between Luxembourg and France.

The girls led the way to the barrier and we all gave up our tickets and passed through without incident. A few minutes' walk brought us to a rather shabby apartment block where the girls handed us over to the occupants of one of the flats and then disappeared. We only slept here one night, then we were passed on to a house occupied by a policeman, who slept on the couch in his sitting-room so that we could have the bedroom. Again it was only a one-night stand and then we spent several days in a big, modern house whose owner was a bank manager.

Here we had every comfort – a splendid room with soft beds and beautifully-laundered sheets, a tiled bathroom with unlimited hot water, and wonderful food. The family consisted only of the bank manager and his wife. They both spoke English, and our stay with them was most enjoyable. The bank manager thought the RAF was marvellous: when the air-raid sirens went, his eyes lit up and he'd say, "Good boys! Now your comrades give the Germans a bad time, yes?" He'd get out a bottle, then down we'd go into the cellar and drink a toast to the Royal Air Force. I remember thinking it would be ironic if we were killed by RAF bombs, but the chances were infinitesimally small, as the aircraft overhead were merely in transit to and from Germany.

We had been with the bank manager and his wife the best part of a week – during which time we were visited by a considerable number of their friends who all wanted to meet us – when they told us one day that we were to cross the frontier into France the following morning before dawn.

VI

Meeting the Duke

When Hitler took over Luxembourg, saying that it was part of Germany, this also meant that young men in Luxembourg became liable for service in the German army. I understand that none of them actually fought against the Western Allies, but certainly some were sent to fight in Russia, which of course was a far worse experience. So when young Luxembourgers were coming up towards conscription age, they used to try to get into France to join up with the Maquis instead.

It was two of these youngsters who came to the house to pick us up and act as our guides. They were introduced to us as Adrian and Michel. We all had a quick drink together before our departure and the bank manager and his wife shook hands with us effusively as we began putting our coats on.

"A little something to keep you warm on your travels," remarked the husband, handing us a bottle of cognac. "I... er... I hope you... I mean..." He seemed lost for words, and we too were feeling a little emotional as we tried to express our thanks.

"After the war, when you are home again, you will write to us?" asked his wife.

"Of course we shall," I assured her. I did too, addressing the letter simply to 'The Bank Manager, Differdange' as they had told me to, but my letter was returned with a note saying that the couple had moved to France and their new address was not known.

Having said our goodbyes, the four of us slipped quickly out of the back door and were away. It was somewhere around the beginning of November by now, so the night was cold and we were glad of our overcoats. It was misty too, which couldn't have suited our purpose better, and it wasn't long before we were well away into the hills. We had been told to be careful because the Germans patrolled the frontier between Luxembourg and France with dogs, but Adrian and Michel strode confidently onwards through the woods and fields, and since Chris and I had no idea at all of where we were or which way we should go, we had no option but to follow.

In the event we had no trouble getting over the frontier. I don't really know how long we walked. It must have been a couple of hours or so after we started that Michel and Adrian said we were in France. Chris and I doubted this and said so, because we hadn't crossed a single strand of barbed wire, but the two Luxembourg boys were adamant.

They were quite right of course: we were indeed in France. Our route brought us gradually down from the hills and on to a country road. Daylight had already broken by the time we entered the first French village.

As luck would have it, there to meet us on the main street was a gendarme, who regarded us with a very suspicious eye indeed. I could scarcely blame him: four young men of military age, each carrying a paper parcel of belongings, strolling down the street of a village near a frontier in wartime at six o'clock in the morning must have looked about as inconspicuous as a battleship. However, he said nothing when we passed him, though it felt as though his eyes were boring into the backs of our necks as we walked on.

Our sighs of relief on turning the corner were premature. We found the railway station and Adrian went to enquire about train times while Michel, Chris and I ordered coffee in the station café, which was crowded with early-morning workmen. We were just settling down at a table when our gendarme friend came in, stumped straight over to us and demanded our identity cards.

Frankly, I should not have been surprised if the game had been up there and then. I don't know what was on the forged identity cards that the Luxembourg boys had, but Chris's and mine described us as deaf and dumb. This was an obvious device to get over the language difficulty if people questioned us, but it did seem to me too much of a coincidence for anyone to swallow that two deaf mutes of military age should be travelling about together. After I had been in France for a few weeks I came to realise that the coincidence must have looked even stranger than I thought, because every British or American escaper or evader I met had the same description on his false identity card. If the Germans had simply pulled in all the deaf mutes passing through their checkpoints, they'd have caught the lot of us! It's always been a mystery to me why they didn't.

To my utter astonishment the gendarme simply gave a cursory glance at our cards, muttered politely *"Merci, messieurs,"* and disappeared.

For all we knew, however, he might have been going for reinforcements, since he was aware there were four of us altogether, so when Adrian returned we decided unanimously not to wait for the next train. We had a fair amount of money that had been given us by the underground and when we emerged from the station and saw a wood-burning taxi parked outside, we piled in and ordered the driver to take us to the next village.

We arrived there without mishap, booked tickets to Paris and reached the Gare du Nord that evening. The train was very crowded and we had to stand all the way, but this was an advantage when we reached the ticket-barrier, because there were so many passengers that the identity check could not be as thorough as it might otherwise have been.

I approached the barrier with Michel, and Chris went with Adrian. Michel and I passed through without trouble, but when Chris showed his identity card to the gendarme, the German soldier standing with the gendarme said something. Adrian had already got through and didn't stop: I don't blame him either. However, Michel had more nerve than any of us and he went back and spoke to the gendarme and the soldier. Whatever he said seemed to satisfy them, and they let Chris go through.

"What was all that about?" asked Chris as we all joined up again and went out into the street.

"He wanted to know where you came from," replied Michel. "I told him Toul, just as it says on your identity card. He asked why you couldn't answer for yourself and I showed him where it says on your identity card that you're a deaf mute."

I looked at Chris, all six feet two of him, with his blond hair and fantastically ill-fitting clothes, looking like a prize-winner from a tramps' ball.

"And he actually believed you?" I said, and shook my head incredulously.

Michel's shrug expressed his contempt. "Damned *Boches*! They believe anything if it's on a piece of paper with a rubber stamp on it!" He changed the subject. "But now, we must get busy. We have to find somewhere to stay the night, because there's a curfew in Paris and if we are not indoors we shall be arrested."

So we walked until we found a shabby *pension* in a row of tall terraced houses somewhere near the Louvre. It seemed a reasonably insignificant place, and time was getting on, so we went in. The proprietor was sitting behind the reception counter. He was an old man with a wizened face and when Adrian said we wanted to stay for the night he took his mucky old pipe out of his mouth and glared at us each in turn, his lip curling a little as he came to Chris and me. I began to feel uncomfortable and it didn't improve matters when a big Alsatian dog lying in the corner opened one eye and began growling at us.

At last the old man quietened the dog, squirted a long stream of black juice into the spittoon at his feet and pushed two forms across the counter at Michel and Adrian, who filled them in and signed them. Chris and I might not have existed for all the notice he took of us.

Then he took down a couple of keys and handed them over to Michel in exchange for some money.

"What happened there?" I asked, as we went up to find our rooms. "He looked as though he knew exactly what we were."

Michel laughed. "Yes, he did. But if we get caught by the Germans he can say that Adrian and I spoke French and our identity cards looked all right, so he signed us in, and that we must have brought you and Chris into our rooms without his knowing."

The beds were a bit rickety, in fact the whole place was, with peeling wallpaper and an old-style ewer and basin on a marble slab, but it didn't stop us sleeping soundly after the busy 24 hours we'd had. The coffee next morning was that dreadful brew of roasted acorns and chicory that they had to use on the Continent during the war, but the rolls and *confiture* were good, and when the four of us emerged into the early-morning streets we were fighting fit again and ready for anything.

There were very few people about as we walked to the Metro station. Down on the platform it was a bit more crowded, and while we waited for the train we got some amusement from watching a tough-looking German NCO with a back like a ramrod giving hell to a scruffy-looking old soldier for slouching down the platform with his hands in his pockets.

The Metro took us to the Gare du Sud, and Michel and Adrian booked tickets for Clermont Ferrand in Vichy-administered France. A gendarme and a German guard were standing by the ticket-collector, and we split up into twos as before. This time we got through without difficulty. The train was well packed, and when I saw an apparently empty carriage about halfway along it, I very foolishly gave a whoop of delight and piled in before the other boys could stop me. This could very well have been our undoing, because I walked straight into the arms of a German soldier. Although I don't speak German I had no difficulty in catching the meaning of his bellow of rage, and I cleared out in rapid style.

"Fool! Fool!" Adrian shot at me in barely suppressed fury as I rejoined the others. The fright and anger battling for mastery of his features were mingled with frustration, for his command of English was quite inadequate to convey what he thought of my rashness, and he could do no more than splutter and gesture wildly.

Michel, on the other hand, who was much better at English and could certainly have found the words to chalk me off, was in no condition to do so: he was helpless with laughter at my discomfiture. This illustrates well the differing characters of our two guides. Adrian was nervy and difficult to get on with; Chris and I had words with him at times and we'd have had more if his English or our French had been better, because of his bad habit of going to extremes. Either he would be super-cautious, so that we all stuck out like joints of beef in a health shop, or he would panic, as he had done in the ticket-barrier incident.

It had been typical of Michel to pull Chris's fat out of the fire at the Gare du Nord; equally typically, he didn't let my blunder disturb his equanimity. When he had managed to recover from his giggling fit he explained what I had done wrong.

"That carriage is reserved for German troops," he said. "There were notices plastered all over it to say so. Adrian's right to be angry really. You could have given us all away. You and Chris simply must stay with us and not wander off on your own. Let us do the leading and you copy our example."

We did in the end discover a compartment in the next coach with four empty seats. Michel and Adrian sat on one side and Chris and I on the other. The train kept stopping and starting in the inexplicable way that trains do in wartime, and it is a long way from Paris to Clermont Ferrand, so the journey was not exactly a hilarious adventure. However, a certain amount of comic relief was provided by a young couple in the compartment who had evidently just got married – or perhaps they hadn't – but nevertheless, the presence of the other passengers did not deter them from enjoying themselves in a pretty basic fashion: in fact, they just about had it off under our very eyes!

If that served as a reminder that France is always France, another minor incident demonstrated that more serious matters were nevertheless not far from the minds of the French people. A few minutes after we had pulled out of Paris, a young Luftwaffe officer came from the coach next door and invited the French passengers standing in the corridor to fill up the empty seats. His offer was obviously well meant, but it was totally ignored. He stood there looking a bit embarrassed, then spoke again. Still no one took any notice, and after a few tense seconds of silence the German went red to the roots of his hair and turned on his heel. I felt very sorry for him because he looked a pleasant enough sort of chap.

We stopped at a few stations and people got on and off, but there was no sort of a check until we got to Vichy, where a gendarme came round with a German officer in tow, who clicked his heels and asked for identity cards. Chris and I were sweating ice-cubes as we handed them over, but after a brief glance the officer handed the cards back with a word or two of thanks. And that was it... not a question, not a stare at any of us, nothing. We were in the clear.

Not long afterwards we pulled into Clermont Ferrand. By now it was late afternoon, and as we walked out of the station Michel and Adrian were in pretty high spirits.

"Nothing to worry about now," they said. "The French are all friendly, and the German troops stick to the airfields and barracks. As long as we don't go asking for trouble, nobody is going to bother us."

Chris and I doubted this optimistic-sounding assessment, but as we discovered, the Luxembourg boys were right. It was true that when the Allies invaded Italy in 1943, the Germans moved into what had previously been Unoccupied France. But they never did take control of the government in the same way that they had in the Occupied Zone. They stationed themselves at the obvious strategic points such as railway and road junctions, airfields, barracks and suchlike establishments, but they made no attempt to take over the administration and left the French almost completely to themselves. As long as the French didn't bother the Germans, the Germans didn't bother them. In effect, the Germans conducted themselves more as troops stationed in a foreign country than as an occupation force. All they were concerned about was to hold southern France against the Allied thrust from North Africa and Italy.

Chris and I only had a hazy general idea of where we were going. We felt very much like a couple of parcels being handed on from one individual to another in a party game. Nevertheless, we were happy enough. For one thing it seemed plain that the risk of being captured was diminishing rapidly with every move we made, and for another, we didn't have much choice anyway: we just had to do as we were told or else we'd be on our own. One thing we were in no doubt about: we were getting nearer to Spain all the time, and we assumed that our ultimate destiny would be to cross the Pyrenees, which we had been told back in England would be one of our most likely escape routes.

Clermont Ferrand is of course a large industrial town, and there were plenty of people about. Adrian and Michel said that we had to wait until dark before our next move, and although they did not think there would be any particular danger in hanging round the streets, it seemed better to kill time in some less conspicuous way. So we went to the pictures and sat through a couple of hours of a terrible comedy film that did nothing at all to relieve the tedium of waiting. We emerged into the unrelieved gloom of blacked-out streets, and a dark figure materialised out of the shadows and accosted us. How he knew who we were I have no idea, but he exchanged a few voluble sentences with Michel and Adrian, who turned to us with cheerful grins.

"It's OK," said Michel, "he's from the Maquis. We have to go with him."

So off the five of us walked, through the suburbs of Clermont Ferrand, into the open country and upwards into the hills. I wasn't keen on this part of it, because it seemed to me we were making no effort to keep off the main roads, but when I pointed this out to Michel and Adrian they told me not to worry and indicated by their attitude that as far as they were concerned our guide knew best. With the benefit of hindsight, I realise that he did too, because the chances of even seeing a German soldier, let alone being challenged or picked up by one, were very remote indeed on these roads. I don't think Chris and I comprehended at this stage just how very much in the clear we were.

We carried on for about an hour in this way, none of us saying very much because the continuous trudging was quite strenuous. Finally, we reached a road junction on a forest-clad hillside where we found another figure awaiting us. This chap turned out to be a middle-aged farmer, and with only the briefest of greetings he led us off along the side-road while Michel and Adrian disappeared in the other direction with our original guide. This was the last we ever saw of them, in fact, and we scarcely had a chance to say goodbye or to thank them for their help in getting us away from Luxembourg.

The farmer had no English and Chris and I still hadn't picked up a great deal of French, but we were getting accustomed to the system by now and we simply plodded along with him until we reached the remote little farmhouse where he lived. We were tired from the day's exertions, but after our previous experiences we fully expected a slap-up meal and soft beds at the end of our journey to make up for it.

We were not disappointed either. The farmer's wife and family gave us an effusive welcome, a tremendous meal washed down with gallons of red wine and the best two beds in the house. The fact that we were getting used to this kind of treatment didn't diminish our appreciation.

Next day we woke up quite late, had a leisurely breakfast and pottered about idly for an hour or two. We agreed that if this was the hell of war, we were all for it. Of course, it couldn't last and at about two in the afternoon we heard the sound of a car approaching. As it drew nearer it became apparent that it was being driven right up to the limit of what tyres, accelerator, brakes and road-surface could tolerate.

"Good God, what's that?" said Chris uneasily.

The farmer came out of the house, gesticulating wildly and gabbling too fast for either of us to understand properly, but he did manage to make it clear that this was to be a big day in our lives. A moment later a big black Citroen bounced up the driveway at tremendous speed, its engine blipping and jets of muddy water squirting up from the ruts in the track. With a squish of horse-dung, it slid to a halt right beside us.

"*Eh bien, il est venu!*" shouted our host as the front passenger's door opened. He made it sound as though it was the Almighty who had come to visit us. In a way, that was not far from the truth.

The man who climbed out of the car to greet us was an astonishing figure. He was thick-set, clean-shaven and about forty years of age. He wore a belted leather jacket, green trousers tucked into the tops of a pair of thick white woollen socks and a pair of hefty ankle-boots in soft, natural yellow tan. On his head was the traditional Frenchman's black beret, and in his hand was something a lot less traditional: a wicked-looking Colt 45 automatic that he waved at us cheerily. He looked like a mixture of soldier, mountaineer, gangster and Pyrenean smuggler – not a bad description really, for as we were to discover, this was pretty much what the Maquis was all about.

"Hello boys!" shouted this fearsome-looking character, his face splitting into a huge grin. "Welcome to *la belle France*! Now everything is all right, no more troubles, no more running away, no more *Boche*! The Duke takes care of everything round here!"

Jeannette, Norman Lee's French girlfriend.

VII

"Un Grand Bordel"

In claiming to "take care of everything" the Duke, as he was nicknamed, was not far from the truth. He was the Maquis boss of a very large area, I believe, in fact, the entire south of France. He made a point of meeting, in person, every British or American escaper or evader reaching his territory – to size them up, I suppose, and to make sure they weren't German agents. His real name was Charbonelle, I heard, and he was reputed to be a millionaire. I don't know whether that was true, but he certainly owned, or at least controlled, a big road transport fleet – a useful asset for the leader of an underground army.

"Let's go inside a minute," said the Duke after we had all exchanged greetings. "I need to ask you a few questions."

So into the farmhouse we went and our host got out the customary bottle of wine. Now in all the films I've ever seen about Occupied Europe, it's at this point that the underground interrogators give the British lads a right old going-over to make sure they aren't *agents provocateurs*. It starts off in friendly fashion, but then all of a sudden the underground leader will bawl some insult at them, slap them in the face or knock them down, giving them a kick or two in the groin for good measure. Provided their screams of agony are delivered in a good Brummagem accent and they can recite accurately the names of their local football first eleven (a thing I've never been able to do), the underground leader is satisfied with their authenticity and everything dissolves into mutual backslapping.

The Duke didn't operate like this at all. He looked at our identity discs carefully. Then he asked if we knew anyone called Ed and Johnny, also from Middleton St George, and on which operation had they gone missing? When we replied "Montlucon" he asked no further questions. Casual though it was, this cursory interrogation was quite sufficient. The Maquis were in continuous touch with London by wireless, and of course all they had to do was to transmit the details from our dog-tags and a short resumé of our account of ourselves. The Air Ministry would confirm the information, and nothing more would be necessary.

The questioning over, the Duke drained his glass and rose to his feet.

"Ready, boys?" he enquired.

So again Chris and I said farewell to our host and hostess – we were becoming pretty good at this by now and were rapidly learning the correct French words and phrases – and out we went to the car.

The Duke gestured in the direction of the driver, a youngish man with a hatchet face and a uniform that was a carbon copy of the Duke's – including the Colt 45.

"You see him?" asked the Duke. "He is the best driver in the Maquis. Before the war he was a racing driver. You will see."

The chauffeur smiled in friendly fashion while Chris and I exchanged uneasy glances, then I shrugged my shoulders. I have always believed that if you can't avoid being raped, you may as well lie back and enjoy it!

Even so, it rocked me a bit when I saw the inside of the car. There were two sub-machine guns on the front passenger seat, a good half-dozen or so hand-grenades at the back, and spare magazines for the tommy-guns littered about all over the place. It looked like a Chicago gangster's back-kitchen.

"We just have to move these things out of the way," explained the Duke hospitably. He and the driver heaped their martial miscellany into corners and onto the floor to make room for us, then Chris and I climbed into the back seat.

Now I've heard it said that other people have cars, but the French are armed with them. This may be a libel on the rest of the French nation, but as far as the Duke's driver was concerned it just about fitted the bill. Corners didn't exist for him: nor did brakes. The Citroen roared and screeched from one hairpin to another, and we'd have been done for more than once if anything had been coming the other way. We found later on that the Duke always drove around like this; and there was method in his madness, for although an ambush by either the Vichy authorities or the Germans was highly unlikely, the Duke's Citroen at top speed would have been a difficult target to hit or to stop in such an event.

The Duke turned and pointed at the pile of small arms as we screamed round a particularly stomach-turning S-bend.

"You boys know anything about these things?" he shouted.

"Not much," yelled Chris. "Norman's the expert on gunnery."

The Duke looked at me enquiringly.

I shrugged my shoulders. "I know how to use a machine-gun in an aircraft," I answered, "and I've shot off a few rounds with a sub-machine gun on the firing range, but I can't say I'm very familiar with them. I've had a bit of instruction on hand-grenades but I don't remember much about them."

"Well, we run into any trouble, you remember damn quick," bellowed the Duke. "First thing you do, you hand those machine-guns up front, then you get down on the floor and give us spare magazines and hand-grenades when we ask for them." He paused and grinned. "But don't worry – no one catches the Duke. The damn *Boche*!" he grimaced with contempt. "He doesn't know where to look, and no Frenchman will tell him. The French police, they do know where to find me – sometimes – but if they come looking for me, they always let me know first. Friendly, eh?"

Chris and I agreed that it did seem a convenient arrangement, and I decided that since the Duke was some sort of a boss man it might be a good idea to try and find out what plans, if any, existed for getting us out of France.

"When are Chris and I going home?" I asked. "And where are you taking us now?"

"Ah," replied the Duke, "you are in a hurry, yes?"

"Yes," said Chris. "We're very grateful for everything that people have done for us but we've been moving about for a month or more. You say we're well clear of the Germans, so shouldn't we be moving off to England soon?"

"Yes, yes," said the Duke, a bit irritably, "I know all that. But first I take you where you meet up with some more RAF boys. Then we wait a few days and an aeroplane comes from England to pick you up. What do you say to that?"

Chris and I looked at one another, all smiles.

"Bloody marvellous!" I said.

A few minutes later we pulled off the road, bounced along a rough track for a couple of hundred yards, then slithered to a skidding halt outside a dilapidated farmhouse. We had arrived at the headquarters of the local Maquis group.

Half a dozen men, all dressed in outfits broadly similar to those worn by the Duke and his driver, greeted our arrival. We recognised two of them at once as Ed and Johnny and Chris and I greeted them like long-lost brothers even though we hadn't actually known each other terribly well at Middleton St George.

As I explained earlier, bomber crews on my squadron scarcely got to know other crews as anything more than vaguely familiar faces, if that, but nonetheless it felt pretty dramatic and pleasing that four of us from No. 428 Squadron should join up together in France like this.

Ed was the flight lieutenant navigator and Johnny a wireless op/air gunner on the aircraft I described earlier as having been bombed from above by a Stirling. The pilot had crash-landed the aircraft and everyone had got out. Some had been taken prisoner by the Germans, but Ed, Johnny, the flight engineer and the flight lieutenant rear gunner (who was also the squadron gunnery leader) had all managed to evade capture and were filtered through to the Maquis by the underground just as Chris and I had been.

This had all taken place about three weeks before. The flight lieutenant rear gunner had injured his back in the crash-landing and the flight engineer had soon begun to suffer from trench mouth for some reason. The French had no means of treating him and he was in a dreadful state – gums rotting and teeth falling out – so in response to a wireless request, a Lysander aircraft came from England and picked up the two casualties.

This sounded very encouraging, because it proved that the Maquis were in touch with London and that people could be got out of France if they had to be. But some time had gone by since then, and Ed and Johnny warned us not to set too much store by the continual promises of the Maquis that an aircraft would be arriving in a couple of days or so.

"Remember we're not far from the Mediterranean here," said Ed, "and people are always trying to convince you that something nice will happen if you'll wait till *mañana*."

He was only too right. We soon met the leader of the group, Doronto, whose assurances were indeed very persuasive. The promised aircraft never did come, but this never embarrassed Doronto or prevented him from making equally fervent predictions for the following night, or the night after, or next week...

The other possible route to England, and the one we had assumed we would be taking ever since leaving Luxembourg, was across the Pyrenees to Spain. But Chris and I found, as Ed and Johnny had before us, that whenever we tried to discuss this possibility with Doronto or the other Maquis people they became rather evasive. The truth was – and in the end Doronto admitted this – that the Germans had cottoned on to the Pyrenees escape route and were making it more and more difficult to use. The climax came when they trapped a big party of Americans making their way across and pretty nearly wiped out the lot of them. After that, they cleared a five-mile belt on the French side of the mountains and established armed guards, dog patrols and all the rest of the paraphernalia.

When word of this reached our Maquis group, it was the finish of our dreams about escaping to Spain, so although we saw it as our first duty to return to England and get on with the war from there, we had reached a full stop for the time being. To begin with it was not too difficult to reconcile ourselves to this. We had evaded capture by the Germans, got through Occupied France and reached at any rate some sort of destination, where we could recharge our batteries for what we believed would be the next stage of our journey home.

Life with the Maquis soon began to fall into a regular pattern – a rather primitive one at first. The group comprised about twenty young Frenchmen as well as ourselves, and we had a deserted farmhouse for our living quarters. It was very ancient and dilapidated and I don't think the group can have been using it for very long before our arrival because they were still in the early stages of trying to make it habitable. We slept on heaps of straw on the floor, which was a bit draughty, so we separated our 'beds' from each other by resting planks on their edges and nailing them into the floorboards. This was a great improvement. One boon we did have right from the start, surprisingly enough, was electricity. The French power-grid is pretty comprehensive, and even though our hideout was miles up in the hills, transmission wires were handy and all we had to do was tap them. This, of course, cost nothing.

The civilian clothes in which Chris and I had arrived were highly unsuitable for this kind of life, and we soon began wearing the same outfit that most of the Maquis boys wore and in which we had first seen the Duke – leather jacket, green trousers, woollen socks and yellow boots. We asked Doronto where it came from, and he laughed.

"The Germans have this civilian labour corps, the Todt organisation: it builds fortifications, airfields, military roads and so on. They conscript young Frenchmen into it – if we don't clear off and join the Maquis first! There are one or two Todt battalions doing forestry work in this area and the clothing the Germans give them is very good, so when we need some, we just break into one of their stores and take it!"

I laughed too, and I find it amusing to this day to think that most of my time on what you might call 'active service' was spent in the uniform of the German equivalent of the Pioneer Corps.

We obtained certain of our other requirements by the same sort of method as our electricity and our uniforms. Petrol, for instance, was no problem at all. Of course the ordinary French civilian running a car had to use one of those charcoal-burning affairs mounted behind the luggage boot or a balloon of gas on the roof, but there was petrol for the Germans, petrol for the French collaborators – and petrol for the Maquis.

The system was simple. When a petrol station received its allocation, the Maquis was informed. We drove quite openly to the garage, collected our 200 litres or whatever we required, paid for it and drove off. The garage proprietor then reported that he had been robbed. The police made a note of it, and everyone was happy. As a kind of bonus, the garageman would generally exaggerate the amount of his 'loss' thus getting himself an additional hundred litres or so to flog on the black market.

An alternative method for obtaining petrol was to take a run down to the nearest rationing office, have a drink and a chat with the official responsible for issuing ration coupons, pay him a reasonable sum of money and come away with as many petrol coupons as we wanted. The official reported them stolen and that was that. We got tobacco and cigarettes by similar means.

Food was a different matter: this we bought in a perfectly straightforward fashion. We got bread from the local bakery, and butter, cheese, meat and potatoes from the farmers of the district, who were friendly with the Maquis and very pleased to do business with them. The populace naturally had good reasons for liking the Maquis, which provided a refuge for those dodging call-up for forced labour with the Todt organisation or in Germany, or for anyone who might be in trouble with Vichy or the Germans. However, it was also in the interests of the Maquis to foster good relations with the local population. If they had bullied or robbed the peasantry they would not have stayed popular for long and the country people knew all the Maquis hideouts and could have betrayed them to the Vichy authorities or the Germans very easily. So there were mutual advantages.

It suited the farmers to supply the Maquis and it equally suited the Maquis to pay fair prices with genuine money supplied from London, but they wouldn't let themselves be swindled. I was present on one or two occasions when a Maquisard had offered a farmer a fair price for a bullock or a pig only to be met by a demand from the farmer for a black-market figure. The Maquisard simply took his gun out and repeated his original offer, thus concluding the deal!

When the food had been obtained it was the Frenchmen who cooked it and we aircrew were very glad to let them do so, because they had the French culinary touch all right. I remember a kind of casserole of rabbit in red wine that still makes my mouth water when I think about it!

All in all, we lived pretty well, and it is a curious comment on the vagaries of human luck that I ate better in Occupied Europe during the war than I did in England when I arrived home again. Rationing was very much of a reality at home, but almost from the moment I was shot down I ate like a king. That does not mean that the food shortages in Europe were not real: even in France there were plenty of people suffering in the industrial towns, but as always happens in wartime, the country dwellers were able to look after themselves.

Of course we aircrew took our share of the chores – chopping firewood or doing odd jobs to improve our living quarters and although we still thought of ourselves as waiting to go back to England, as the days slipped by we unconsciously became more and more assimilated as members of the Maquis group. We wore the same clothes, shared the routines and duties, made trips to the local market town (though we were never allowed to go unaccompanied) and of course we were picking up more and more of the language. It wasn't long before I became pretty fluent and I had an opportunity of showing my proficiency one day when the Duke came over on one of his visits. He liked the British, and especially the RAF, and he always made a point of chatting with us. On this occasion he happened to ask me what I thought of the Maquis, and I replied in good French slang, *"Ce n'est qu'un grand bordel!"* – which, literally translated, means, "It's just a big brothel" but as far as I was concerned meant "What a bloody shower!" The Duke slapped me on the back and laughed till the tears ran down his face.

But that was my serious opinion. The Maquis didn't seem to do anything, and a lot of our time was spent idling. We'd collect a bit of firewood, wash the dishes, go for a walk, drive into town, or just sit around drinking seemingly endless supplies of *vin ordinaire*. It was obvious that a good many members of the group simply fancied themselves as gangsters, especially the younger ones around my own age. They swaggered about with revolvers in their belts, took little care of their weapons, did no sort of training and were not in any sense a disciplined fighting force, although Doronto did keep pretty good day-to-day control in a rough and ready kind of way.

I realise now that I was doing the Maquis a certain amount of injustice. Louis, a young schoolteacher in the group who used to practise his English on me, explained it to me one day.

"You English only want to fight the Germans," he said, "and of course we want to defeat them too. But you have your government helping you: they organise your efforts. Here in France, our government helps the enemy. So we have to fight our own government as well as the Germans."

"All the more reason for getting on with it then," I replied.

He waved a hand in the air. "Pouf! How are we to do that? A dozen or two of us riding into Clermont Ferrand in lorries to attack the German barracks with revolvers and fists? And will your British army come across the Channel to help us?"

"No, of course not," I admitted, "but we do help you in other ways. Where do the Maquis get most of their money and weapons from? The British and Americans send them."

"Yes, they do," he retorted, "and we shall know how to use them when the time comes. But first we must organise."

To be fair, that is what they were doing. The Maquis originated as an anti-Vichy movement, and as long as it seemed to be a matter of French internal politics, the Germans were glad enough to let well alone, even though they knew the Maquis wanted ultimately to be rid of them just as much as of the Vichy government. The German objectives in southern France were strictly limited, and their troops were thin on the ground, so it was left to the gendarmerie and the *milice* – the Vichy equivalent of the Gestapo – to deal with the Maquis. They made occasional sweeps as a matter of form, but since the gendarmerie invariably gave the Maquis advance notice, these were naturally not very successful.

This freedom from interference enabled the Maquis to grow stronger and become better organised. More young men were joining it all the time; weapons and money were being parachuted in from England and North Africa; men like the Duke travelled about coordinating the groups and setting up a chain of command; and General de Gaulle's Free French headquarters established overall command from outside. There was never any question of the Maquis acting as an 'underground' movement, sabotaging and harrying the Germans as used to happen in the parts of Europe directly under military occupation and control. Its policy at the time I joined it was to wait and prepare, and there is no doubt that this paid off. By the early summer of 1944, when D-Day was imminent, the Maquis was a powerful army. The attacks it launched on the Germans were an enormous help to the Allies. But more than that – and this was clearly what de Gaulle was after – the French population was so much on the side of the Maquis and the Vichy administration and police were so riddled with Maquis sympathisers, that the whole collaborationist régime crumbled to dust. Of course the Vichy government would have fallen anyway with the departure of the Germans, but the point was that the *Forces Francaises de l'Intérieur* (the title de Gaulle gave to the Maquis) were able to fill the political vacuum at once and sweep de Gaulle himself straight into power.

This all looks very obvious now in the light of later events, but it was by no means so clear-cut in the winter of 1943/44. The French political situation was very confused indeed at that time. The North African landings had brought General Giraud on the scene as a rival to de Gaulle, who, as everybody now knows, had a knack of exasperating Churchill and was, frankly, detested by President Roosevelt. Moreover, the communists were very powerful throughout the Resistance, both in Occupied and Unoccupied France and their plans for postwar France were very different from those of the remnants of the pre-war political parties, which were also jockeying with one another with an eye to the future and blaming each other for the past. Finally, there was still a dwindling band of Frenchmen (though I never met any) who believed the Germans were going to win – or were so tarnished by past collaboration that they had to believe it.

Thus de Gaulle, who at that time had no more justification for his pretensions to be the supreme leader of the nation than had a good many of his rivals, was playing a waiting game. This was not only the correct military strategy while awaiting the Allied invasion, but also gave him time to plan a way to create out of the political chaos the kind of postwar France he wanted.

A couple of weeks or so after we joined the Maquis group, I acquired a girlfriend. One Sunday, Doronto took Johnny and me into the local market town to spend an evening with a family he knew. The father was a former captain in the French Navy and Doronto told us he had invented the magnetic mine, though I don't know whether this was true. At any rate, he was most affable with us and I got on with him famously. He was a bit sore about the sinking of the French fleet at Oran by the British, but admitted that it had been necessary to take some kind of action because of the situation that existed at that time. His daughter's name was Jeannette, and she was a typical French provincial girl; rather on the stocky side, to tell the truth, but fresh-faced and with a lively personality.

There was just one awkward moment during the evening. It came after dinner, when Johnny remarked that he was hot, translating it literally into French: *"Je suis chaud."* The mother removed Jeannette from the room immediately, leaving the captain to explain to Johnny that when a Frenchman uses those words he means he is randy!

Of course the explanation brought smiles all round, but it is a fact that middle-class French families in those days were somewhat on the stuffy side and had a rigid code of conventions. Jeannette's mother gave us a splendid meal and was very kind, but it was clear that she ruled the household – and also that she wasn't too keen on Doronto. The French middle class looked down somewhat on the working class, and Doronto couldn't have been mistaken for anything else.

Still, we had a most enjoyable evening, and for my own part I hit it off extremely well with Jeannette and her father, even if not so much with the mother.

A day or two later, I had a surprise when one of the boys came back from a run into town. When he got out of the car he was carrying a small parcel.

"I've got something here for you, Norman," he called.

I opened the parcel. Inside was a pair of socks – which I badly needed just then – and a silver cross of Lorraine, the symbol of the Free French. Jeannette had sent them to me.

Doronto was looking on. "So that's it!" he exclaimed, grinning from ear to ear. "Little Jeannette fancies a bit with Milord Anglais from the RAF, does she? Just be careful her old hag of a mother never finds out, that's all!"

From then on, inevitably, Jeannette was regarded as my girl, and I suppose you could say she was, though I never did take advantage of her – not that her mother would have given me the chance anyway. But I did visit the family a lot, and every time I returned from one of my calls Doronto would ask me if I'd laid Jeannette yet. I've no doubt he would have liked me to, just to spite the mother. Sometimes when I couldn't get into town for a few days Jeannette would write me a letter, and the French boys in the group used to concoct all sorts of things for me to write back. It all helped to pass the time in a light-hearted sort of way, but circumstances were really against its developing into anything very serious, partly because of Jeannette's family background and also because I still thought I was only in transit on my way to England.

Our progress in that direction was nil, however. On the day Doronto told us that the Pyrenees route was shut, he took me down to an *estaminet* in the town and we got completely plastered. My recollection of the evening is very hazy, but I do know that at one point he was chasing two girls around a table, roaring at me to catch them at the other side so that we could rape them. I'm sure he would have, too, if I had complied.

However, I can't honestly offer the excuse of drinking to drown my sorrow at not being able to cross the Pyrenees. I got drunk simply because I wanted to get drunk. I still believed – and the French boys kept asserting it – that sooner or later an aircraft would come to take us out of France.

This was at least part of the reason for the cold reception we gave to a proposition put to us by the French boys at about this time. A British aircraft on an arms drop to the Maquis had been shot down. All the crew had been killed except one, who got away safely but was picked up by a gendarme who happened to be a collaborator. He handed him over to the Germans. The French suggested that sometime when this particular chap was known to be on duty we aircrew might like to take a run down to the village gendarmerie in the car and toss a couple of hand-grenades through the window. We told them in no uncertain terms that this was not our idea of how we ought to fight our war.

In any case – although we were too tactful to make any reference to the fact – we had on the strength someone else who seemed to us rather more suited to this kind of task. This was a young man whom we nicknamed 'Fred'. God alone knows what his real name was; we never asked. No one ever asked anything much of Fred or talked to him at all if they could help it, because it was plain that Fred's only interest in life was his Luger, which he scarcely ever stopped cleaning. He looked and acted just like a gangland hit-man in a Hollywood film. We were convinced that he was a Maquis executioner.

Now and then Fred would wander off on his own. Nobody knew where he went and nobody followed him. We never discussed these mysterious absences with the French, but the circumstances coinciding with Fred's final vanishing trick convinced us that our assessment of him was correct.

General de Gaulle told the Maquis that anyone who killed a collaborator would be paid some kind of reward or bounty. Immediately after word of this offer reached us, Fred disappeared from our group. We were sure that he had gone off to earn himself some bounty in Clermont Ferrand. When he failed to return we surmised that he might have been caught by the Germans, who had rapidly initiated identity checks and anti-Maquis searches in the big towns as soon as they heard of the bounty system.

In my view this move of de Gaulle's did no good at all. It encouraged bad feeling between Frenchmen, of which there was more than enough already, and the settling of personal scores. Any collaborators who were thus assassinated at de Gaulle's instigation could have been dealt with equally well, and in a more orderly fashion, after the war. It also roused the Germans against the Maquis to no purpose.

The sharpening of the German attitude was illustrated for us in another way at this time. One day the Duke came on one of his visits. He was grinning from ear to ear as he got out of the car.

"Here, boys," he shouted. "Come and look at your photographs: tell me if you think they're any good!"

He spread out a poster for us to see. There we all were – the Duke, his driver, Ed, Johnny, Chris and I, with a reward on our heads. The photograph was one that had been taken on one of the Duke's many visits. No doubt it was an indiscreet thing to have done, but the Duke was very proud of his RAF boys. I am not certain how it had got into German hands, but it is possible that the Duke's first driver, who had been captured by the Germans, had had a copy of it on him.

"There, you see..." the Duke slapped at the poster contemptuously, "the *Boche* thinks you boys are all my personal bodyguard. How do you like your new careers as French gangsters?"

The Duke was clearly in high good humour about it all, and I can't say that the thought of being a wanted man upset me particularly.

"Where did you get hold of this?" asked Johnny.

"Down at one of the gendarmeries when I dropped in for a drink," replied the Duke in great glee. "It's stuck up everywhere in this area – in police stations, post offices, on hoardings – all over."

"Fame at last," remarked Chris, a little sourly, "but all the more reason for getting the hell away from here. When is the aircraft coming for us?"

The Duke sighed and looked serious. He spread his hands and made the usual sort of response.

"I don't know," he said. "Perhaps a day or two more. It is very difficult. Try to be patient. We do our best."

"A pity it can't be a bit better," commented Chris.

The Duke shrugged and turned to me. "What's the matter with him, Norman?" he asked as we strolled away.

"Nothing really," I replied. "You mustn't take too much notice. Chris is living for nothing else but that aircraft. He doesn't seem to be able to take things as they come the way I can. Not," I added hastily, "that I want to stay here for ever either."

"No, I understand," said the Duke. "I understand very well, but no one can make miracles. An aircraft will come soon. That's all I can say."

These conversations always ended inconclusively, but I didn't let it get me down. After all, we were safe, we had shelter, we were well fed and watered, we were with friends – even including, in my case, a girlfriend. No doubt we would get to England eventually. Meanwhile, why fret over things we could do nothing about?

VIII

Winter

More days went by. It was well into December and had been snowing hard when the local gendarmerie gave us the tip-off to move, because they were going to have to raid our hideout. The Germans had learnt where our group was located and had passed the information to the gendarmes (as if the gendarmes didn't know perfectly well already) together with a very clear suggestion, which couldn't be refused, that something needed doing about us.

Our new location was to be a bit further up into the hills, about fifteen miles away. We had to shift the bits and pieces of furniture we had acquired and the radio. Our transport consisted of a big van and that was all. Doronto and one or two others were to go with the transport and the rest of us were to march.

The move was to take place in the evening. While we were packing up it became apparent that there wouldn't be room for everything in the van. One of the things that we had to leave out was a barrel of wine. We were determined not to waste the wine, so we all got stuck into it and in no time at all the packing of the van resolved itself into a glorious booze-up. Some were singing; some were crashing into one another with the chairs they were carrying; all, I regret to say, were thoroughly drunk. If the gendarmes had really wanted to take us, that would have been the time. Half a dozen determined schoolboys could have rounded us all up!

Now I must confess that I was about the worst of the lot, and the moment eventually came when I began to feel really bad, so I got up and went outside the house, wandered about a little and finally sat down on the running-board of the van, sweating and shivering simultaneously. A couple of the others came looking for me and took me in again. They sat me in the kitchen and forced black coffee into me, and ultimately I started to come round.

At this point Doronto said it was time for us to begin the journey.

"OK," said Chris, "but what about Norman?"

"What about him?" retorted Doronto with a shrug. "He marches, the same as we arranged."

"Oh, do I?" I butted in. My condition had improved sufficiently for me to feel aggressive in the face of what I regarded as victimisation, but by no means enough for me to enjoy the prospect of a fifteen-mile hike. "And how are *you* travelling?"

"I'm going with the van," replied Doronto. He had had a fair whack at the wine too, and his voice began to rise. "You know quite well what the arrangements are."

"Yes, I know quite well how *you've* arranged things," I retorted nastily, "so that *you* don't have to walk. But if a bloody Frenchman is going to ride, then you can bet your life I'm riding too."

And with that I sat down. If Doronto had chosen to have a showdown – which he had every right to do as leader of the group – an unpleasant situation might well have developed. But Ed and Johnny and Chris intervened to cool me off, while Doronto agreed that after depositing the contents of the van at our new hideout he would drive it back along our line of march and pick up the walkers.

So off went the van with Doronto and a couple of helpers. The rest of us started walking, and I was by no means the only one who was unsteady on his feet. It was bitterly cold and the slush was thick on the road, so it would not have been a particularly enjoyable evening's stroll even if we had been stone-cold sober.

After we had covered some distance, one or two of us – and this certainly included me – began to sag. It was still not terribly late, and as we were passing a farmhouse with chinks of light showing from badly blacked-out windows, Louis, the young schoolteacher, suggested we should ask the occupants to let us come in for a few minutes' rest.

The family welcomed us warmly when he explained who we were. The two young daughters in particular were thrilled to bits when they discovered that four of us were from the RAF. They gave us coffee and wanted to make us a meal. In trying to explain that I wasn't hungry, I translated literally from English and said, "*Je suis plein*." This threw the girls into hysterics, because what I had said does not mean "I am full" but "I am pregnant"!

We were sorely tempted by the hospitality offered by the family, but after drinking our coffee we felt we must push on again. I reckon we had covered five or six miles altogether by the time the van arrived back to pick us up.

Our new home was not very different from the old. Indeed, on the basis of the experience I acquired with the Maquis, I can tell you that when you've seen one deserted farmhouse you've seen them all. This one was slightly bigger than the previous one, which was a good thing, because the group was getting bigger too. But there were still the same holes to mend in the floorboards, the draughts to stop, the radio to rig and the electricity to pinch before we could call it home.

We stayed a long time in this new location, and frankly, it got to be very boring. Once we had got the house fixed up there was little to do. Our incessant nagging at the French about an aircraft to take us home produced nothing but irritated half-promises, and they disliked us going for walks on our own, for which I don't blame them. The snow got higher and our spirits lower. It didn't help matters either that the Duke's visits became very infrequent for a while, perhaps because of the weather.

Chris seemed to take it particularly badly. He couldn't seem to get on with the French and made no effort to learn the language or take part in such activities as were going on. He stood his share of guard duties, of course, and occasionally chopped a few sticks of firewood, but that was all. He was just waiting to go home.

I could sympathise with him, but I couldn't share his approach. I never worry about things I can't change, and I couldn't just sit about moping, so Chris and I became less close as time went on, particularly after a couple more fliers, Eric and George, came to join us. They had been shot down over Luxembourg even before us, so their movement down the pipeline had been very slow. Eric

Brearley and I chummed up and got into the habit of going on foraging expeditions with Louis.

These trips relieved the tedium of our situation greatly: they also helped to make me fitter than I had ever been as operational aircrew. We'd slog hard all day, sometimes through snow that was waist-high, wandering from one farm to the next to see what they could sell us.

We always armed ourselves with revolvers and perhaps a Sten-gun for these expeditions. This would have deprived us of the protection of the Geneva Convention if we had been caught, but this didn't worry us for five minutes, any more than it did when we were doing guard duty at night. There was no likelihood of German troops venturing into the hills, especially in winter.

Our arms were largely a matter of form, and we didn't expect to use them on these trips. Certainly we took no precautions whatever in approaching farmhouses. We knocked on the door, announced ourselves as members of the Maquis to whoever answered it, then waited for the wine to flow, as it never failed to do. We generally came back at the end of a day's foraging with a fairly heavy load on, of drink if not always of food, because when Eric and I were introduced as members of the RAF the farmers would make a tremendous fuss of us. We would have a long chat over a bottle, or several bottles, before starting to bargain about food. The talk nearly always turned to politics, and naturally the French always reproached us for 'deserting' them at Dunkirk or for the attack on their fleet at Oran, but although we argued about this sort of issue, there was no question that we were on the same side, fighting the same enemy. We never had the slightest fear of these people betraying us to the Germans or the Vichy authorities.

It was during this period that a serious disciplinary incident occurred. One of the Frenchmen stole a revolver from another. The heinousness of the crime was magnified by the fact that we were still short of weapons and were using all kinds of museum-pieces. Doronto dealt with the thief swiftly and ruthlessly. First he beat him up, then he flung him into a windowless storage cellar for a week on bread and water. The worst part of the punishment, however, was that on being released from his confinement the offender was expelled from the group. To be thrown out of the Maquis was pretty tough, because you then stood an excellent chance of being picked up by the Germans unless you could do some very fast cross-country work and bluff your way into another Maquis group where you were unknown.

Not long afterwards the gendarmerie tipped us off to move again. We had barely settled ourselves into our third deserted farmhouse before they advised us to move yet again. None of these moves was a matter of more than fifteen or twenty miles or so, and we were never very far from Clermont Ferrand. From where we lived, in fact, we had a grandstand view of the night raid in which the RAF destroyed the Dunlop factory at Clermont Ferrand. The praise which the French showered on the RAF about this was very gratifying. They told us that the factory had been taken out "like a slice of cake" and that there was scarcely any damage to civilian property at all. As aircrew ourselves, familiar with the difficulties of accurate bombing at night, we too could appreciate what an achievement it was.

It was at our fourth location that changes began to occur that brought the organisation of our group on to more formal military lines. The first was that we had an arms drop, so that for the first time we had plenty of modern weapons to go round. There were not only revolvers but Sten-guns and hand grenades – more than enough, in fact, for our own needs, so we were able to pass on the surplus to other Maquis groups in the vicinity.

Secondly, the accommodation here consisted of two houses, and since the group had now grown to about forty men in all, distinctions of rank and function began to appear. The 'other ranks' moved into one of the houses, while Doronto picked out a number of the older hands, including all the RAF element, to occupy the other house with him as 'officers'. It became understood that when we gave orders the 'other ranks' carried them out. They would stand up when we entered their quarters, and they didn't come to ours uninvited. What I did appreciate about my new status was that we 'officers' no longer did guard duty. Stamping my feet in the snow while clutching a cold Sten-gun has never been my idea of a hilarious way to spend the hours of darkness.

But the winter days and weeks slipped by and still we remained essentially passive despite these changes. We foraged, we played cards and chopped wood, we stripped weapons. I wrote letters to Jeannette and she wrote back. One day she and her family actually came on a visit, but when she asked me to take her for a walk and show her the forest, we didn't even reach the door before her mother stopped us.

The boredom got worse and worse. For a long time the Duke didn't show up at all, and since it was he who generally supplied our tobacco we were reduced to blending our dwindling stocks with hazel-leaves and all kinds of rubbish in a coffee-grinder.

Then one day we heard a piece of news that really got us off our backsides. A message reached us from the town that the Duke had been taken by the Germans. Doronto called an officers' conference at once, and we tried desperately to think of something we could do. Of course there was nothing, and we had no choice but to fret uneasily while waiting in hopes of further information.

It came a day or so later. The Germans hadn't got the Duke after all: from what we heard it was more the other way round, but he had been wounded and was now in a 'safe house' in Clermont Ferrand.

I had never seen Doronto move so fast. In a couple of minutes he had detailed a couple of men as escorts, piled into a car with them and disappeared in a spurt of gravel.

The car was back within the hour. From the back seat emerged the Duke, grey-faced and with his arm in a sling, but smiling. We took him into the house, and he sat down and told us what had happened.

"It was about a week ago when I was travelling along the main road just outside Clermont Ferrand. Maurice was driving as usual. Well, everything was quiet and there was no other traffic about, but suddenly we saw ahead of us a small open military lorry with eight or ten German troops in it, moving very slowly in the same direction. It was too good an opportunity to miss. I told Maurice to pull alongside the lorry so that I could spray them with a tommy-gun. Well, Maurice swung out on the overtaking side, and as we got parallel with them I gave them a couple of heavy bursts. A lot of them went down and the lorry stopped. That was where it went wrong. Maurice was supposed to stop too, as close to them as possible, so that we could finish them off quickly. But he put the brakes on a bit late, and when we came to a halt the range was too long to be sure of killing them all. By this time some of the Germans had recovered themselves and began firing at us. I shouted to Maurice to get started again, and as he did so the bullets began hitting the car. One of them wounded me in the arm, as you see." He grimaced.

"We drove into Clermont Ferrand at a hell of a speed, dumped the car in a back street and went to a safe house. The doctor came and fixed me up. After that I just rested until Doronto came for me."

This incident did not dampen the Duke's high spirits or enthusiasm. Nor, on the other hand, did it signal any change in the general Maquis policy of lying doggo. The Duke's attack was quite unpremeditated: all it amounted to was that he saw a sitting duck so he took a pot-shot at it. Neither our group nor any of the others that I heard of would have been strong enough at this stage to undertake a sustained hit-and-run campaign against the Germans. Had we tried it, the Germans would very likely have put the pressure on the gendarmerie and *milice* to take more effective measures against us. They might even have undertaken punitive expeditions themselves despite their shortage of numbers. They did organise an occasional sweep even as it was, and we would hear now and then of some Maquis group having been wiped out as a result.

One of these instances came to our notice through a mysterious character who was brought in one day by Doronto. This chap claimed that he was a South African with the RAF and had been shot down in the raid on the Dunlop factory in Clermont Ferrand. He had evaded capture, so he alleged, and had found his way to another Maquis group which he had now left because, for some vague reason, he "didn't get on with them". Doronto was suspicious of the man's account of himself and asked us to interrogate him.

We had no doubt the man was South African. He had a 'Japie' accent you could cut with a knife. Nevertheless, we shot a large hole in the rest of his story within five minutes. He claimed to have been flying Mosquitoes. We asked him to describe the Mosquito. The details he gave in reply were all authentic – but they applied to the Liberator, not the Mosquito.

At this point he admitted that his story of having been shot down over Clermont Ferrand was untrue. In fact, he said, he had been in the South African army. Although his appearance did nothing to indicate the fact, he was a Cape Coloured. The South Africans did not arm coloured troops but only used them as labourers. He was taken prisoner by the Germans at Tobruk. The Germans had used Cape Coloured prisoners as labourers but had segregated them from the whites and treated them well. He had eventually found himself in a camp near Paris, going out to work daily almost like a civilian and being allowed a great deal of freedom of movement. Ultimately he got bored and simply pushed off, made his way south and joined up with a Maquis group. He had been unhappy with this group, partly because of one or two individuals whom he couldn't get on with, partly because the group had no other English-speaking members and he felt isolated.

"OK," said Ed at the end of this recital. "But it would have saved a lot of trouble if you'd told the truth in the first place. Why didn't you?"

"Would you?" was the simple reply.

We felt that this was a fair comment. We knew that coloured troops in the South African and American forces suffered a lot of humiliation and our new acquaintance may have hoped, by suppressing his origins, to avoid facing any more. We were satisfied, too, that the large chip he carried on his shoulder probably explained his difficulty in settling down with other people.

Certainly, his behaviour, after we had, with difficulty, persuaded Doronto to accept him, confirmed that the South African was an awkward cuss. He refused to move in as an 'officer' with the rest of the aircrew but took up his quarters in the 'other ranks' house. As an 'other rank' he went on the guard duty roster and was doing a stint on the evening Doronto received word that the Maquis group he had previously been with had been wiped out shortly after he left it.

Doronto wasted no time. "We're taking no more chances with him," he said, "Norman, you and Claude go get him over here right away. One of the boys from the other house can take over his guard duty. Then I want him interrogated again – thoroughly this time."

I got up. "He's bound to ask why we're bringing him in," I said. "What do we tell him?"

"Tell him he's under arrest and make him hand over his gun," answered Doronto. "If he resists or makes any kind of fuss, shoot him. Don't argue, just kill him."

I'd never done anything like this before, but I had no doubt Doronto was right, and anyway he was the boss. So Claude and I cocked our revolvers and went out. We disarmed the South African without difficulty and returned with him to the officers' quarters.

Again we interrogated him, going over the same ground as before. We spent a couple of hours at it, and all of us had a go – Ed, Johnny, Chris, Eric, George and me – but we couldn't make a dent in his story. We got a few more circumstantial details to fill it out, but nothing that was inconsistent with the line he had adopted during our earlier interrogation of him.

The only slightly suspicious answer we got was when we insisted on knowing the full reasons for his having left his previous Maquis group.

At first he would only repeat his earlier assertion that there were one or two individuals in the group whom he couldn't get on with. We were determined to have something more solid than this, and in the end he rather grudgingly said that they had abused him and knocked him about because he was coloured.

We interpreted this to Doronto and he gestured impatiently. "But that must be a lie," he cried. "Frenchmen don't ill-treat coloured people just because they are coloured."

Now, generally speaking, I believe that Doronto was right, and we said so to the South African. He shrugged his shoulders stubbornly. "I can't help what the French usually do. I only know what these Frenchmen did to me."

"Pah! He's lying," said Doronto, contemptuously. "And if he lies about that how do we know he's not lying about everything else? But what we do know is that as soon as he left that Maquis group, it was wiped out by the Germans. Someone must have betrayed them. If he didn't, then who did?"

It was Ed who, as the senior aircrew officer, had taken the leading part in the interrogation, and he broke in at this point.

"I'm sorry, Doronto," he said firmly. "I don't go along with you, and I don't think the rest of us aircrew can either. I admit the circumstances look suspicious, but you can't shoot a man on suspicion alone. We've interrogated him twice. All six of us have had a go at him, and his story stands up."

"His first story didn't," objected Doronto. "So there's one clear lie we've proved."

"We went through all that before," said Ed. "We were satisfied with his explanation then and there's nothing new to show why we shouldn't be satisfied now."

"Except that the Maquis group he left got wiped out," retorted Doronto.

"All right," said Ed. "What are you going to do then? You're the boss. I've told you what I think, and the same goes for the rest of us too. Our opinion is he's clean. But it's up to you to decide."

"You can't shoot him because he doesn't like the Maquis," Chris put in. "Otherwise you'd have had to shoot me by now. All you've got against him is suspicion. Why don't you just chuck him out of the group? Let him go free but chuck him out?"

"Because it we let him go free he can betray us, that's why," replied Doronto.

"Well, what then?" asked Ed.

Doronto pondered in silence, then turned to his French lieutenants. After a few minutes of voluble discussion he addressed us again.

"All right," he said. "We'll give him one more chance. You keep a very close eye on him, Ed, I'm relying on you. The first suspicion you have, you tell me – the very first, remember. I'm not having us all endangered for the sake of one man."

Three days later the South African went missing. Some items of clothing were missing from the 'other ranks' house at the same time. Shortly after that Doronto said casually one day: "Oh, by the way, some of the boys found that South African friend of yours who absconded with the clothes. They shot him for stealing. Just as well, really. I still think he was a German spy."

I said nothing, because there seemed to be nothing to say.

IX

Spring

The execution of the South African, like the wounding of the Duke, reminded us that a grim reality lurked behind our day-to-day routine and that in the end, the game was going to be played for keeps. Undisturbed as we were in our mountain fastness, it was impossible for us to maintain a sense of high drama through the succession of grey winter days. It was with great relief that we noticed at last the hours of daylight lengthening and the thaw setting in.

The springtime sense of awakening and expectancy showed itself in a number of ways. Almost before the snows had melted we were swimming in the waters of a dam nearby. It was ice-cold, but we were pretty hard by now and none of us minded, although the leeches did put me off a bit. The French, on the other hand, didn't seem to worry about the leeches in the lake: they used to laugh at me for being so sensitive. Nor did they worry, I may say, about the bugs that plagued us all constantly through sleeping on straw. Whenever we became infested we aircrew would boil our clothes and have a bath-night with kettles of boiling water in an old cauldron. The French thought this was terribly funny and made no attempt to follow our example. Even Louis joined in the general derision, so one day we decided that anyone who spent as much time with us as he did ought to be as clean as we were so as not to contaminate us. We got the cauldron going, grabbed Louis, stripped him and flung him in. Then we gave him a right old scrub-down while he cursed us in not quite correct English ("bloody rotten fools and hellfire bullies!" etc) and the other Frenchmen laughed their heads off. Poor Louis didn't get his clothes back until we'd boiled them. After that, the French still jeered at us on bath nights – but from a safe distance!

Another sign of spring appeared when I came out in a rash of heat-spots. This was normal for me at the change of seasons, but Doronto was very worried and took me to the hospital in town, where a lady doctor examined me. After looking at the spots on my arms, chest and back she asked if I had any more.

"Yes," I replied, "between my legs."

"Take your trousers down then," she said.

That did it. I flatly refused to do so and we left, Doronto shaking with merriment over my Anglo-Saxon prudishness. He took me to another doctor – a man this time – who was delighted to meet a British flier and accordingly began by prescribing a bottle of wine for the three of us. After half an hour or so of chatting he sent us away with several boxes of multi-coloured pills, and for the next few days Doronto fussed about like an old woman making sure I took them conscientiously.

The significant point about my visit to the doctor, however, was that it was quite openly made. Theoretically, we were all liable to be shot if caught; Doronto and I for carrying weapons and the doctor for aiding the Maquis.

You would not have thought so to see us drinking and joking together in the doctor's surgery with no attempt at concealment. We felt perfectly safe. For by this time the population of Vichy France was overwhelmingly pro-Maquis, and the collaborationist régime was helpless to do anything about it because too many of its own servants and functionaries were pro-Maquis as well. The Germans, fighting to stem the Russian tide in the East and preparing to meet the forthcoming Allied landings on the Atlantic coast, could not spare the strength to sit properly on the lid of the French kettle.

As the spring progressed our group continued to grow, and our discipline stiffened further. The division of functions became more and more clear-cut. I stopped foraging for food, for example, this was not an officer's job, nor did I think it any part of my job, officer or not, to be subservient to a Frenchwoman who joined our group for a few days about this time. She was a courier whom the Duke employed for carrying messages between the Maquis groups he controlled. The Germans were thought to have a line on her, so the Duke had decided to hide her up for a while until the heat went off. No doubt she was doing a dangerous job for her country, but she seemed to think this gave her the right to boss everybody around. After all, I thought, I too had done and was doing some dangerous things for my country, so it looked like level pegging, and I had no compunction about making plain that her attitude wouldn't wash with me. It was just as well that she left fairly soon, otherwise there could have been real trouble.

We had always listened to the BBC news on the radio, of course. In particular, if Mr Churchill was due to speak the group would drop everything except guard duties to listen to him. One day, among the code messages relayed at the end of the news bulletin, there came one that quenched all our remaining hopes of returning to England. This was an order from the Air Ministry that shot-down aircrew in France were to stay put; they were not going to evacuate any more of us. We were to remain in France and instruct the Maquis in the use of the weapons that were now arriving in ever-increasing quantities. The Maquis was to build itself into a disciplined force, capable when the time came of striking blows that would be coordinated with the operations of the Allied invasion forces.

Some of our aircrew were very disappointed about this. I was too, in a way, but on the other hand it was a relief to be told clearly what was expected of us. There could be no question that the decision was a sensible one, so it didn't take me long to conclude that the shortest way home was to get on with the job that had fallen to us.

The need was there all right. We were getting Brens, Stens, lots of old Lee-Enfield rifles and Webley .38 revolvers, plenty of ammunition, and hand-grenades by the score. Instruction books were dropped too, but although these were in French as well as English, no instruction book seemed capable of impressing on the Maquis the importance of keeping their weapons properly cleaned, so we buckled down to the job of convincing them, and gradually the results began to show. The men began to look and act like soldiers; they got to know their weapons; we set up an impromptu firing-range and got some proper shooting practice. We mounted stronger guards, enforced a stricter discipline and established regular routines and procedures. Doronto drove us instructors hard, and we drove the men. The Duke was as pleased as punch with our progress.

We were busy, then. We had an aim in life, and we were beginning to feel confident of achieving it. The Maquis was becoming an army.

It was sometime in April, I think, that the Maquis received the order to begin forming themselves into larger units. This meant that our group must move again. By now a change of location was a full-scale military operation. There were at least fifty of us in the group. We had a car and several lorries and vans at our disposal – and we needed them, not only to transport ourselves but to shift the large quantities of bedding, camp furniture, stores and above all weapons that we now possessed.

It may have been quite safe or it may have been foolhardy, frankly I have no idea, but the fact is that we moved in broad daylight, with no attempt at concealment. What's more, our destination was a location on the other side of the town of Le Puy and although we had heard there might be German troops in the town our attitude was "so much the worse for them". Our column drove straight through the town centre, a carload of men armed to the teeth leading the way and the heavy transport following filled with equipment and cheering, singing Maquis, uniformed and brandishing their weapons. Those who saw us would have had to be blind and deaf not to know what we were.

The citizens of Le Puy knew all right, and they waved and shouted "*Vive le Maquis!*" as we rumbled past them. It was an exhilarating experience – until the van I was riding in had a puncture right in the middle of the main street. Yet it scarcely dampened our spirits. The rest of the convoy carried on, and we pulled off into a side-street garage, watched approvingly by smiling passers-by. We took the precaution of closing the doors and setting a guard while the garageman fixed our tyre, but neither he nor we felt any particular apprehensions about our presence being observed. A few minutes later we rattled out again to catch up with the convoy. If there were indeed Germans in Le Puy, they kept well out of our way. I dare say it was just as well – though whether for them or for us I'm not sure.

The rest of the journey, which amounted to fifty or sixty miles all told, was uneventful and brought us to yet another hilly, densely-forested tract, the site of a large Maquis encampment. A good many other groups had already arrived and were well organised. The headquarters was a big farmhouse in a central clearing, and the various groups were dotted about in huts and tents in the surrounding woods, forming a rough perimeter. All the groups guarded and patrolled their own sectors of the encampment, which I estimate must have contained about a thousand men.

We six aircrew were split off from our own group at this stage to form up into a separate contingent with a number of other English-speaking escapers and evaders who had already arrived. We made a fair-sized party: four British, four Canadians, five Americans and an Australian. Another half-dozen or so Americans drifted in over the next week or two.

We were quartered in a rough wooden hut with bunks down the sides for sleeping. It was rather crude: something like the accommodation you see in POW films. We had no blankets, but there were plenty of parachutes, which made an excellent substitute. The sleeping accommodation was roughly partitioned off from a kind of living-room, and we had a lean-to shed as a kitchen. Lanc, one of the RAF evaders, took charge of the cooking, and he was marvellous. With his primitive old wood-stove he turned out first-class meals: at my suggestion he even had a go at Yorkshire pudding, and although he was a Londoner he made a splendid job of it!

As a self-contained group, we now did our own catering, and it was no longer regarded as necessary for us to be escorted by a Frenchman when we went out. I was glad to resume foraging, because our instructional services seemed not to be required and time began to hang heavily again.

Eric Brearley and I used to go out together on these expeditions, usually accompanied by Johnny, who spoke Québecois French, and Buck, the Australian.

Buck was a cheery character and very good fun to be with. He spoke no French worth mentioning, but this never deterred him from enjoying life or making sure of getting what he wanted. What he wanted was generally "*du fromage jeune*", meaning a local young farm-cheese of which he had become very fond, and his earnest face and determined manner of repeating these three words over and over would send the French farm-people into fits of laughter. Whenever he wasn't after *du fromage jeune* Buck would be after something to drink.

This presented little difficulty: there was plenty to be had. (When I come to think of it – and as you will have gathered – I can remember scarcely any period during the whole of my war service when there wasn't plenty of drink to be had of one sort or another.) We were returning one night about eleven or twelve o'clock from a day of foraging that had been marked by even greater hospitality than usual on the part of the farmers we had visited. Buck was so drunk that he could scarcely stay upright, and he wouldn't stop burbling nonsense at the top of his voice – in English of course. The rest of us were sharing his load of victuals between us and doing our best to help him along, but we were unable to prevent him from suddenly falling into a gully with a bloodcurdling yell.

The disturbance Buck caused frightened the Maquis perimeter pickets, who mistook his English for German and alerted the defences. The guard turned out armed to the teeth, and we were lucky that they challenged us on our approach instead of shooting first and seeking explanations afterwards, which was the more usual Maquis method of solving mysteries.

By this time, actually, it was not really all that necessary to go out foraging at all: we did it to pass the time as much as anything. There was generally plenty of food to be had from the headquarters, which was about 45 minutes walk from our hut.

Johnny found one day that something else was to be had from there too, if any of us had fancied it: a young girl whose head had been shaved as a collaborator. She had been held prisoner and thrown to the troops, and Johnny was told she had been had by eight or ten Maquisards the night before. He was then offered a turn, which he declined tactfully. The girl herself was all in favour of attaching herself to him as a means of getting away from the French: she thought the Anglo-Saxon group might treat her less brutally. We agreed with Johnny's decision to leave her alone. At its crudest level there was no knowing what she might have caught from all the Maquisards who had raped her. For another thing, there was no knowing what trouble the presence of a woman in the group might cause. Finally, and perhaps most important of all, it was none of our business, because it was not our country that had been invaded by the Germans.

This incident was a sign of the times. The French were not waiting for D-Day to start paying off their scores; the Maquis were in firm control of large areas, and rough justice was being meted out in the villages. Many women were shaved bald and many men were shot.

There was every reason to hate the Germans of course; for example, a Frenchman who had been in Gestapo hands showed me his nail-less fingers and the whip-scars on his back. But it was hard to know whom to trust. On another occasion, a driver and escort were sent out to bring in a Frenchman who had asked to join the Maquis. On the way back he pulled a gun and killed them both.

Another Maquis car was following behind, however, and the occupants took him alive. He was lucky to get a swift bullet.

Not far away was a small hamlet that was a nasty sight. The buildings were burnt-out shells. Not a living soul remained. The Maquis had been accustomed to use it, drinking at the café and buying food from the shops. One day a German punitive expedition had arrived, shot one or two of the inhabitants, ejected the rest, and set fire to their houses.

The pot was coming to the boil. As far as we evaders were concerned, the most exciting piece of news was when we heard of the arrival by parachute of a liaison team consisting of a British major, an American captain, a Free French lieutenant and a wireless operator. We were naturally agog to meet these chaps – and were correspondingly crestfallen when we did, because they displayed no interest in us at all. Their business was to organise the Maquis, and that was all they cared about. Perhaps it was as well, because we should not have taken kindly to it if they had conceived the same idea as some of the Frenchmen had had about us earlier on. In view of our skill as 'weapons experts' (which in truth we weren't) they had wanted us to form what they called an élite assault squad to lead their forthcoming attacks on the Germans. We had declined the honour very promptly and firmly, pointing out that we were not infantrymen and that in our opinion it was more fitting for Frenchmen to lead in the liberation of French territory.

Altogether this was a strange period. On the one hand I could not help being aware that the tension was mounting, on the other I was doing nothing and felt like a bit of a spectator. Loafing, foraging and reading – God knows where all the English paperbacks came from, but they always came – were not really enough to fill our time.

One day the tedium was relieved by an invitation to a village wedding. I've never seen such an orgy. A lot of Maquisards were there, the bridegroom was a member, and a good share of the population of the village turned up. All were dead drunk when we arrived. It didn't take me long to catch up with them, so my recollection of the occasion is necessarily hazy. However I do recall that, for some reason I could not fathom, the bride and groom were not speaking to one another the whole time I was there. The villagers were all wearing *sabots* (clogs) in which they performed a noisy dance around a lot of empty bottles arranged in intricate patterns on the floor. When I left after 36 hours, exhausted and totally incapable of further debauchery, the celebrations were still in full swing and apparently continued for another two days!

A second memorable break in routine occurred when Ed and Johnny went out one night with an arms-drop receiving party. When they came back they were very glum, and we asked them what was the matter.

Ed's voice shook now and then as he told us. "Well, when the aircraft came on the run-in we signalled with our torches as arranged. We saw the parachutes coming down spot on target, but he was hellish low. I was talking to the pilot over the walkie-talkie and I kept yelling at him to climb. It all happened very fast, but he seemed a bit lost

– I don't think he realised how low he was. Then we heard a horrible smashing sound in the distance, and then nothing – just silence. He must have flown straight into a mountainside. The French reckon there's not a chance of locating it until daybreak."

Word reached us shortly after dawn that the wreckage had been found. All the crew were dead of course; their bodies had been extricated by the inhabitants of a town nearby who passed the word over to our group.

A party of us went over in a lorry, and as we drove into the town square we saw a mass of people assembled before the *hôtel de ville*, taking their turn to crocodile slowly into the building like Russians visiting Lenin's tomb. Inside were six coffins – we thought there ought to have been seven crew and a dispatcher, but the French had only found six bodies – before which the visitors bowed, curtseyed, prayed, or just stood in silence.

The most astonishing feature, however, was the guard of honour. This consisted of half a dozen or so young German soldiers, all very smart and very respectful, standing rigidly to attention under the supervision of a couple of gendarmes. These were motor-cycle dispatch-riders who had been ambushed one by one by the Maquis over the previous few weeks. They were held under guard in a house in the village. The inhabitants felt that the funeral of the British airmen provided a good opportunity for the prisoners to reflect upon the subject of war. Accordingly, during the three days that the bodies lay in state, the Germans were paraded behind the coffins for four hours every morning and four more every afternoon, while villagers flocked from miles around to pay homage.

The sun shone gloriously on the day of the funeral. Just about the whole population of the village came and there wasn't enough room for all of them in the church. The village band, wearing colourful uniforms, turned out, and the fact that they didn't know *God Save The King* and had to play *The Star-Spangled Banner* instead did not detract from the dignity of the occasion, any more than did the Stars and Stripes in default of a Union Jack. We knew the people's feelings were sincere and deep. Even if we hadn't known it before, it was made plain by an incident that occurred as the crowds were dispersing from the churchyard afterwards. One of the Maquis came over to us.

"Here, take this and look after it," he said, handing a wristwatch to Ed.

"Where did this come from?" asked Ed.

"It belonged to the navigator of the aircraft," answered the Frenchman. "You can give it to his family when you get back to England."

Ed pocketed the watch. "Where did you get it?" he enquired.

"When we arrived at the site of the crash, we caught a farmer nearby with this watch. He admitted he had stolen it from the wrist of the dead navigator. So we took it from him."

"What will you do about the farmer?"

"We've already done it. We shot him."

The rest of the day, I'm afraid, contrasted more and more starkly with the solemnities of the morning. A tremendous feast had been laid on in the *estaminet*, and the occasion steadily degenerated into yet another of those glorious piss-ups which all too often seem to have punctuated my adventures in France.

Not that I feel we were displaying any disrespect towards the dead. Speaking from my own knowledge of wartime aircrew, I can pretty well guarantee that the occupants of the six coffins would have been delighted, only regretting that they could not participate themselves. I dare say the same would apply equally to aircrew today.

It was just before dawn one day that we awoke to the faint rattle of distant rifle-fire. We sat up in our bunks and asked each other uneasily what was going on.

The answer seemed only too obvious. At last, after the weeks and months of preparation and anticipation, the pot had boiled over, although not in the way we had expected…

We had thought that *we* were going to attack the Germans. Instead, they were attacking *us*. By forming up into larger groups, the Maquis had given the Germans something to have a go at. Now they were having a go.

X

Break-Up

That the Germans meant business was quickly confirmed by a runner who arrived shortly from headquarters to order our group in from the perimeter. We didn't need to be told twice. At headquarters, we found a scene of controlled confusion. Orders were being shouted and men were bustling here and there with messages and equipment, but there was no panic. The Maquis were clearly determined to put up a stiff resistance.

They did too. The Germans were using SS troops with tanks in support, yet the Maquis, despite their lack of regular training, held them at bay with small arms alone. All day the fighting continued without a pause, and as far as we could tell from the noise of battle and the occasional snippets of information we got from runners, the Germans were making little impression.

As the day went on, we of the English-speaking group discussed rather indecisively between ourselves what should be our own course of action. There were eighteen or twenty of us: four British, four Canadians, Buck the Australian, and the rest Americans, including a USAAF major. We were unanimous that we would not voluntarily involve ourselves in the battle. We were aircrew, not infantry. Weapons instruction was one thing, fighting was another, and the latter had not been included in the terms of the Air Ministry order to remain with the Maquis. But apart from that decision, there was nothing we could do to control the course of events. So we waited.

It says much for the tenacity of the Maquis that they held out, despite the disparity of weapons and numbers, for three days and three nights of almost uninterrupted fighting. It couldn't go on for ever, though, and at about ten o'clock on the third evening of the battle the French told us that the defences were crumbling so we must pull out. They said the group intended to re-form at another location after the departure of the Germans and suggested we should head in the direction of the assembly area.

We hurriedly collected together what food and spare clothing we could carry and set out. The first job was to get rid of our weapons. The Germans had broken into the perimeter in strength by now. If we ran into them it would be pointless to put up a fight, so our weapons would be worse than useless – they would get us shot for violating the Geneva Convention. Not wanting to leave them for the Germans, we buried them some distance away in the woods.

Then we began moving in the general direction the Maquis had indicated. This was not easy, because we had no compasses, and we couldn't see to read the maps given us by the Maquis. Moreover, we couldn't use the roads but had to go cross-country, sticking to the forest wherever possible. Now and then we heard bursts of rifle or machine-gun fire, the grinding of tanks or the shouting of men. We saw several villages in flames.

But we were lucky. We didn't see a single German, and the navigators in our party succeeded in keeping us on a rough course by the stars. By dawn we were clear of both the perimeter and the attacking Germans, and by about eight in the morning, when we stopped in a clearing to rest and discuss our next move, we must have been ten or fifteen miles from the scene of battle.

We opened our packs of food and breakfasted on bread, cheese, sausage and whatever else we had managed to bring away. The American major had taken charge and, quite rightly, would allow no cooking because the smoke might give away our position, so it all had to be cold. But the wine we washed it down with – there was always wine from somewhere! – warmed us, and when the major called us to order for a council of war, I for one felt ready for anything.

"Well, I don't need to explain the situation," he said. "You all understand it well enough, so we can make this quick. Do we head for the new Maquis assembly area or don't we? And if we don't, what should we do instead?"

"Not the new assembly area anyway," said one of the other Americans. "The Maquis group has broken up, and what good do we do them or ourselves by sticking around while they re-form?"

There was a chorus of assent, except for a couple of other Americans – and Chris, of all people. He looked doubtful. "The Air Ministry orders were for staying with the Maquis," he pointed out.

I spoke up. "Yes, but that was when there was a group of Maquis to stay with. It was all right with the first mob: we needed them because we couldn't have fended for ourselves in the winter, and they needed us as weapons instructors. There's no point to it now."

"That's right," said Eddie. "What good will it do to join up with them again? They didn't use us as instructors once our group had joined up with the big one. So in that case what *are* we doing? Surely not waiting for an aircraft to pick us up, because that's one thing we know isn't going to happen."

"And we don't intend to be part of the Maquis army fighting the Germans," put in Eric. "We already decided that three days ago when the battle started."

"I vote we push on," said Johnny. "Head for Spain or somewhere."

"The Spanish frontier's been sealed off," objected Chris.

"All right then, what about Switzerland?" I asked. "What's the matter with Switzerland? That's near here as well, isn't it?"

"OK, hold it," said the major. "One thing I think is clear. The break-up of the group creates a new situation, and most of you RAF people seem to think you're no longer bound by your orders to stay with the Maquis. I must say I agree. I think we have to use our own initiative, make a new decision based on our own assessment of the circumstances. But I don't think we're bound to move as a party either. Maybe we would stand a better chance if we split up, either as small groups or as individuals, all going their own way."

And after some further discussion, that was what we agreed. We formed ourselves into groups according to the direction in which we intended to move, the major seeing to it that each group had at least one map and one member capable of getting along in the French language. We made a fair divvy-up of the food, spare clothing and such other equipment as we had been able to bring away, and then we all set off in our various directions without further waste of time.

It was at this point that Chris and I finally separated. His decision seemed strange to me after his impatience to get away from the Maquis, but he joined up with three Americans who had decided to head back into the woods from which we had just escaped. I thought it was suicide and said so, but their argument was that the Germans couldn't hang around for ever, and that once they had gone the group could emerge from hiding, re-occupy their old positions, then have another think about the future. What all this boiled down to, in my opinion, was postponing a decision that ought to be taken now. Anyhow, they paid the price, being captured by the Germans almost as soon as they went back into the woods. Chris spent the rest of the war in a POW camp in Poland. After the war he returned to England where he married Johnny Harkins' sister before being repatriated to Canada.

Another group, which included Ed, Johnny and George, decided to make for Spain. My own party consisted of Eric, two of the Americans and me. There wasn't really much to choose between Spain and Switzerland in terms of distance, but the Spanish route was said to be blocked by the Germans, and Switzerland did seem a little nearer as well. So we plumped for Switzerland.

Before moving off, our party of four sketched out a plan of campaign. We had no compass, but our Michelin map was first-class and showed every road right down to dirt-tracks. We saw that we had something like a couple of hundred kilometres to cover as the crow flies. Taking into account that the winding of the roads would become more and more severe as we got into the Alps and that we would have to keep to secondary roads and dirt tracks, we realised that our actual walking distance might well turn out to be twice what it looked at first sight, and much of it over hills and mountains. Even then, we might not be able to cross at the first point of the frontier we happened to reach.

This did not daunt us greatly, though it is not a programme I would care to tackle today, because by that time we were hard as nails (I never had a cold all the time I was in France). Our only worry was that our boots wouldn't stand the strain. We were not troubled about money. Eric and I still had our escape-money, incredibly enough, and the Americans had a certain amount too. But we didn't reckon on needing much. We didn't expect to be staying in hotels, nor would we be buying a lot of food. We had plenty of American K-rations and we had little doubt that we would be offered an occasional meal by well-disposed French civilians.

"How do we move?" one of the American boys asked, "By day or by night?"

"Oh, daytime," replied Eric decidedly, and I agreed with him. "Navigating at night would be hellishly difficult, and Norman and I have been in France long enough to be able to deal with the people we meet."

"What happens if we run into any Germans?" asked the second American.

"We're not very likely to if we stay off the main roads," I said. "And if we do, we ought to spot them from far enough away to be able to keep clear. Even if we're challenged we have our false identity cards, and as long as you two keep quiet, Eric and I may manage enough French to bluff us through."

"What? With 'deaf mute' on all our cards?" asked the American.

"Well, it might just work," I said. "But anyway that's not going to happen. The important thing is to cope with the French, and since they're all friendly – even the gendarmes at a pinch – we'll be all right."

The Americans glanced at one another briefly, then nodded agreement. "Suits us," they said. "The quicker we get to the frontier, the quicker we get across it, and that's what we want."

All the groups were ready to move off by now, so without further waste of time we wished the others luck and set off.

Our first day was not a very energetic one: we had already been walking most of the night and by mid-afternoon we were pretty well fagged out, so we found a farmstead in an isolated locality and knocked on the door.

The old chap who answered looked at us rather dubiously, as well he might considering our villainous appearance. Our Todt organisation outfits were combined with odd remnants of our RAF and USAAF uniforms. We carried a miscellany of shabby packs containing our belongings. Our faces were grimy from the past eighteen hours' exertions. Two- or three-day beards completed the picture.

"What do you want?" he asked.

We had already decided that no good purpose would be served by evasiveness, so our prepared speech was straight to the point.

"Good afternoon. We are American and British fliers," Eric announced boldly. "We are walking to Switzerland. May we sleep in your barn tonight?"

The old chap grinned broadly and burst into a noisy volley of excitable French. After six months in France, Eric and I hadn't expected anything else, but the farmer's enthusiasm came as a surprise to the two Americans, who were recent arrivals and had never previously moved beyond the Maquis camp area.

The farmer and his wife would have put us up in the house, but we had already decided that we would not accept this unless we were in a town. Although a visit from the *milice* or the Germans was extremely unlikely, it was still a possibility, and in that case the family sheltering us would be shot. If we were sleeping in a barn or outhouse, however, the family could pretend they knew nothing about us. So into the barn we went and slept like babies.

Next day we covered something like forty kilometres, scarcely seeing a soul and keeping well clear of those we did encounter. Again we found a farmer who let us stay in his barn overnight. This became the normal pattern of our march. Once or twice dark came upon us before we had found anywhere to sleep: we then simply curled up in the open. When we were doubtful of our way we would ask somebody, a woman if possible, because they were made of stronger stuff than some of the men. One old farmer we approached for directions trembled so much that he couldn't hold the map straight to show us, but none of the women seemed afraid: they would smile, shake our hands and chat with us a bit about our adventures before sending us on our way.

The city of St Étienne provided the first upset in this pleasant routine. The approach to the city from the west was across the river Rhône, and we could see no real alternative to using the bridge. Swimming the river was out of the question and it seemed unlikely we could row a boat across undetected even supposing we could find one to steal. A discussion of the problem with a passer-by did nothing to relieve our gloom, for his opinion was that we had no option but to go straight through the city. He also warned the two Americans, incidentally, that they would not find themselves too popular in St Étienne, because it had been bombed by American aircraft the previous day. Not a single bomb had fallen anywhere near the marshalling yards, which were the putative target and which the French would not have minded being bombed. Practically nothing had been hit but private houses and a lot of civilians had been killed. No doubt this was one of those unfortunate mishaps which occur in war, but of course you couldn't blame the inhabitants for being unable to take it so philosophically.

Still, there was nothing to do but push on. "The only thing is," I said, "do we go through now or wait until dark?"

"Wait till dark," said Eric.

"Oh heck," grunted one of the Americans impatiently, "let's just go ahead. We'll probably get lost in the dark, and if we run into some policeman or a German patrol we'll be right up the creek. If we walk straight through now there'll be plenty of people about and nobody'll notice us."

"Right," said the other American. "They'll be too busy clearing up the mess from the bombing to worry about us."

"Unless they ask us to join in and help," I retorted. "Then you two will look a bit silly."

But in the end Eric and I had to agree that on balance the Americans were right. There were risks either way, but without a guide to lead us down side-streets we would be infinitely more conspicuous at night.

The bridge was a long, narrow affair. To our amazement it turned out to be quite unguarded, although we did observe a good few off-duty German soldiers among the numerous pedestrians, cyclists and horses and carts that were crossing it in both directions.

We joined the stream of traffic without hesitation and reached the other side safely, but there were so many German soldiers about that we still felt very nervous. Seeing a small café a few hundred yards beyond the bridge, we decided to go in for a beer in the hope that by the time we emerged the soldiers would have gone. The café-owner didn't have any trouble identifying us, and he didn't beat about the bush.

"Eh bien, bonjours, messieurs les aviateurs Anglais," he greeted us genially. *"Qu'est ce que vous désirez? Peut-être quelquechose à manger?"*

With that he swept us into the back of the house away from the café and served us with a slap-up meal – without charge. He called in one or two of his cronies, opened a bottle of wine and discussed what to do with us.

"There are many *Boches* in this town," he grumbled disgustedly, "and some collaborators as well. You had better stay here in the house till nightfall, then we shall take you through the town and see you on to the right road."

And that was what they did. A guide took us through the back-streets after dark and out into the open country east of the city. After this, we felt that the worst was over. Next morning the sun was shining, trees were budding and birds were singing. Our spirits were high and we all agreed that there were many worse ways of spending the war than on a walking tour of France. The two Americans let their high spirits run away with them, however. As we were approaching the next village they suggested abandoning our customary cautious tactics.

Eric and I still believed we should skirt round all centres of population unless we had some positive reason for entering them; but the Americans were so intoxicated with our success in St Étienne and at the Rhône crossing that they were now all set to go bald-headed straight down the main road.

"Hell," said one of them, "the way you guys want to go it'll take a month to get to Switzerland."

"Maybe it will," rejoined Eric, "but one month doesn't matter when you've been waiting six already, just as long as you get there in the end."

"Well, *we* haven't been in France six months," argued the other American, "and we don't aim to be either. Five gets you ten we can all be in Switzerland in a week if we just keep going. What do *you* say, Norman?"

"I say nuts!" I replied. "We've taken risks when we've had to, and got away with it too, but that's no reason for taking risks when we don't have to. Eric and I have been in France longer than you and we know best. I'm not doing it your way, and that's flat."

"Same here," said Eric.

"Well, maybe we should split up then," said the Americans stubbornly.

So we did. We divided up the remainder of our food equally, then the Americans strode cheerily down the main road while Eric and I stuck to the hills. They told us we could keep the map, because they wouldn't need it.

They didn't either… we heard later from the Maquis that they had been picked up by the Germans in the next town.

I don't remember how many more days we walked, but we pressed on steadily and without running into any trouble. Now and then we might cautiously enter a small village and get a cup of coffee or buy razor-blades or a bar of soap. The proprietors never had any difficulty in spotting us for what we were. Either they would chat with us about the progress of the war, wish us luck and perhaps offer us a drink, or else they would give us our requirements quickly and bundle us nervously out of the shop. Either way, few would accept payment.

The only memorable incident that occurred was when we were compelled to pass through another town. It was night-time and we met up with a Frenchman who passed us on to a friend of his, a university professor. This chap was an ace at chess and I think it was his discovery that Eric could play the game that caused him to insist on our staying several nights in his house. Every now and then Eric would have to leave the chessboard for a breather and then the old boy would teach me. I got tired of him always winning, however, and in the end I told Eric we'd have to get out of the place or I'd go off my rocker. Ever since then I've disliked chess.

Eric agreed that playing chess, sleeping indoors and getting no exercise were no way of preparing for whatever Fate might have in store for us at the frontier. So we hardened our hearts, said goodbye to the old professor and his chessboard, and a few days later had reached within a day's march of the frontier, somewhere near Annecy.

At this point, our good fortune began to desert us at last. First, we ran out of tobacco and cigarettes, then the food and money began to get short. Worst of all, however, the long spell of glorious weather that had favoured us throughout our march so far, came to an end. For two nights and a day it teemed with rain and, as luck would have it, we could find no sort of shelter from it. By the morning after the second night of the downpour we were feeling more than a little sorry for ourselves as we trudged along, soaked to the skin, stiff with cold, hungry and bedraggled, our conversation reduced to monosyllabic grunts.

Our glum half-stupor was suddenly broken by the rustling of foliage, the scuffing of heavy boots and a shouted challenge. Four figures emerged from the forest adjoining the road and ranged themselves across our path. Even without the familiar black leather jackets and yellow calfskin boots it would have been difficult to mistake them for anything but Maquis, since they were all four armed with Sten-guns at the ready position. One of them waved us to a halt.

"Who are you?" he called.

"English, from the RAF."

"What are you doing here?"

"Trying to get to Switzerland."

"Where have you come from?"

"Near Clermont Ferrand. We were with a Maquis group after being shot down. Then the Germans attacked and broke up the group. We've walked here."

The leader came forward and peered at us more closely. "You are not Germans yourselves, perhaps, coming to spy on the Maquis?" he enquired pugnaciously.

I shrugged my shoulders. "You can check our story if you like."

"Oh don't worry, we shall. Meanwhile you come with us."

He turned and spoke in low tones to one of his subordinates, who set off walking down the road.

"Where is he going?" I asked.

"For a car."

"Can you give us a cigarette? We've run out."

He handed us one each and we lit up gratefully.

"Where are you taking us?"

"You'll see."

Twenty minutes later a battered black Citroen roared up. With a Frenchman on either side of us, Eric and I were not exactly comfortable on the back seat, but the journey was short. A few minutes of hard driving brought us to a small mountain town – some sort of skiing resort, I should think. The car squealed to a halt outside a large house near the town centre.

The four Maquis escorted us into the house and knocked at a door on the ground floor. A voice called *"Entrez!"* and we went in. Seated at the far end of the room was a man in his middle twenties or so, wearing British battledress with "Canada" shoulder-flashes and a lieutenant-colonel's badges of rank; an oldish British army captain was standing beside him.

The colonel looked enquiringly at the Maquis leader. They conferred rapidly in French. The half-colonel turned to us.

"OK..." he said in English that was strongly Canadian-accented. "Tell me all about it."

Eric Brearley and Norman Lee (on holiday after the war).

XI
Apéritifs and Eau De Vie

Our interrogation was brief. Our accents were a help, because the captain, whose name was Montgomery, came from Manchester and was able to confirm that we sounded like true Northerners. They accepted us as genuine without waiting for our identity-disc details to be confirmed by wireless from London.

From this point onwards our four Maquis escorts were all smiles. At the colonel's bidding they fixed us up with accommodation in one of the numerous *pensions* near the town square. On the way we passed the local police station, outside which the Maquis paused to show off to us their proudest possession, five German prisoners, who were just beginning their daily work-task. This consisted, believe it or not, of running up and down a short hill all day under supervision of an armed guard. Anyone who flagged or collapsed under the strain was kicked up the backside until he got going again. Eric and I gulped a little at this, and I asked what the point was.

Our guide smiled. "It keeps them occupied so that they are too tired to try to escape," he explained.

"But you could prevent them escaping by keeping them locked up."

He shrugged. "Yes, perhaps. But it is also necessary to remind them that they have no right to be in France. Therefore we treat them less kindly than we treat good French criminals."

The Maquis next took us to the best hotel in town and there left us to our own devices. This was where the colonel had said we would be having our meals with his team, comprising a couple of Free French lieutenants and a sergeant wireless operator in addition to himself and Captain Montgomery. While awaiting their arrival for lunch we settled ourselves in the bar, and I can remember remarking as we sat in our tattered Todt organisation uniforms, sipping delicately at a Pernod apiece, how rapidly the fortunes of war can change. A couple of hours earlier we'd been dog-tired, hungry, out of fags and unable to get in from the rain. Now it seemed we were in for a spell of the life of Reilly.

The fact that we must have been the scruffiest pair of customers the hotel had ever seen didn't give us a moment's anxiety. It did, however, seem to worry a number of expatriate Britishers, about ten or a dozen of them, who used to live in or hang around the hotel. They had been living on the French Riviera before the war, and except for one girl in her twenties they were all getting on in years – which explains why the Germans hadn't bothered interning them when they moved into Vichy-controlled France. However, the Germans wouldn't let them stay on the coast and made the Pétain government evacuate them inland. The men seemed to be retired majors and ex-Indian civil servants, while the women had tweed skirts, hats like baskets of fruit and perhaps a tiny pension or a few remnants of gilt-edged stock left them when their husbands died. The war had blocked all their pensions and dividends, however, and by this time they were looking very seedy. I believe they were actually living on some sort of meagre pittance doled out from Vichy. Eric and I would have felt sorry for them if they had given us a chance, but unfortunately, the social distinctions they had grown up with still seemed to rule their attitudes. They accepted the lieutenant-colonel, presumably because they felt he was of their own class, but they made it plain that NCOs with northern accents were unfit for anything more than a cold "How do you do?" A wet-haddock handshake or even just a nod was followed by a total freeze-out as they turned away and resumed their interrupted conversation with what they evidently considered to be their equals and our betters.

This infuriated us, not only because it seemed ludicrous for people in such reduced circumstances to try to maintain class barriers that had lost all meaning, but also because of their attitude to the war. Not surprisingly (as I have come to realise since then) they wanted a quiet life. Of course, they hoped the Allies would win, but they wanted that to happen somewhere else, not in this nice, quiet little town where you could pull the bedclothes over your head. Naturally, they didn't want the horrid Germans – but they didn't want the horrid Maquis either, because the horrid Maquis might stir up the horrid Germans. Besides, a lot of the Maquis were uncouth, some were criminals and all of them were troublemakers who might wreck the chances of 'respectable' people being able to sit the war out undisturbed while other people won it for them elsewhere.

Eric and I, in our grotty uniforms supplied by the Maquis, carrying dangerous-looking pistols also supplied by the Maquis, and using vulgar French slang taught us by the Maquis, were about as welcome as a couple of Alsatians in a cats' home. I can understand now, looking back, that we could scarcely have expected anything different, human nature being what it is, but to ask me to approve of their behaviour would be too much.

However, I must add that there was one shining exception among this feeble little crowd. He was a retired lieutenant-colonel of the Indian Army and looked the part. Colonel Bogey, we christened him, but our respect for him was profound and we took care to show it at all times. He was even more destitute than the others and rarely came to the hotel for meals. It was clear that he couldn't afford to. He generally ate with the Maquis. Indeed, he spent most of his time with them, running errands and carrying messages on his bicycle, doing odd jobs of any sort. Nothing was too much trouble where the Maquis were concerned. I think they saw more of him than they did of the real colonel who was supposed to be organising them. Although of course Colonel Bogey himself never spoke about it, Eric and I heard from the townspeople that the reason he was the most poverty-stricken of the expatriate Brits was that instead of hanging on to what bit of capital he had been able to preserve, he had spent it on helping the Maquis. Among the whole bunch, he was the only one with the right idea about the war. He was also the oldest and the most infirm. I would put him at nearer seventy-five than seventy. It would be nice to think he got some recognition after the war for his efforts; he certainly wasn't getting any from his compatriots.

At the other end of the age-scale was the young English girl already mentioned, who seemed to have difficulty in recognising our existence. We soon realised that she was contributing to the war effort by sleeping with the French-Canadian colonel, which I suppose might be described as 'aiding the morale of the fighting men'!

Of course, this was none of our business, but it was difficult not to feel contemptuous in the light of the self-evident fact that her precious colonel wasn't fighting very much, and that whenever he wasn't with her he was working off his excess energies at the town brothel. Captain Montgomery, his second-in-command, who was pleasant and efficient and took good care of Eric and me in the short period we spent in the town, was undertaking the real business of organising the Maquis.

There wasn't a great deal for us to do. We were not Army and we were not really Maquis. We didn't mind helping Captain Montgomery or Ted, the sergeant wireless operator, with any odd jobs that needed doing, but we had no intention of being treated like dirt by the colonel and told him so on the only occasion he tried it. We would doubtless have found ourselves a slot in the organisation had our sojourn continued for any length of time, but we felt we had earned a rest after our hike, and apart from one day when we accepted an invitation to an aircrew funeral in one of the hill villages similar to the one we had attended while with our former Maquis group, we were content for the time being to shuttle in leisurely fashion between apéritifs on the hotel terrace, meals in the dining room, and long, luxurious lie-ins in our soft feather beds at the *pension*.

A few days later our interlude of hotel-living without bill-paying was brought to a dramatic end. Eric and I were sitting one morning at a pavement table in the town square drinking coffee. A convoy of lorries came rattling past, filled with excited Maquis armed to the teeth. We asked what was going on and were told that a German force was advancing up the valley towards the town. The Maquis were going out to win a famous victory.

I looked at Eric. "What should we do, do you think?"

"Finish our coffee, I reckon," said Eric. "There's nothing else we can do until we see what happens."

At that moment we heard the unmistakeable engine-roar of a couple of fighter aircraft at full throttle. That was enough. We dashed for the cover of the hotel lobby, pausing there only long enough for our eyes to confirm what our ears had already told us. I remembered quite enough of my aircraft recognition training to know a pair of FW 190s when I saw them. They were diving between the steep valley-sides for a low-level attack on the town.

It was all over very quickly. For a few seconds the sound of their cannon thumped out through the crescendo scream of engines and slipstream, then they were away, climbing like hell to clear the mountain-slope at the head of the valley. They didn't come back and I don't blame them, because with topography like that it was a tough target. But why they didn't have a go at the lorry-loads of Maquis who were already on their way down the valley road I can't imagine. Perhaps they failed to spot them; but certainly the Maquis could scarcely have failed to spot the fighters, or at least hear them. This should have served as a warning that the German expedition against the town had been carefully prepared.

A couple of hours later Eric and I were again taking our ease with a few drinks at a pavement-table outside our *pension* – there was nothing else we could do – when the Maquis lorries reappeared. They were moving a damn sight faster than they had when going out, and they swept past us and straight out at the far end of the town without any of their occupants bothering to reply to our shouted enquiries as to what had happened.

What had happened was all too obvious, however, and it was equally obvious what was going to happen in the very near future. After the departure of the lorries a sort of deadness hung in the air. A swift reconnaissance of the hotel, the liaison team's house and our pension, all deserted, confirmed our sudden suspicion that we were on our own. With its inhabitants vanished like conjurers' canaries, the town resembled the setting for the climax of a Western movie. Even had we not been befuddled by drink, Eric and I would not have fancied ourselves as the lone heroes of a shoot-out on Main Street, and within seconds we were stumbling unsteadily up the road in the wake of the Maquis lorries.

We got clear of the town and began negotiating the upward curves of the road. Then a series of sharp reports made us jump.

"What the hell's that?" demanded Eric.

"Rifle-fire, I should think," I answered. "In the town, from the sound of it. Maybe some of the French have stayed to take pot shots at the Germans."

"They're nitwits if they have," said Eric. "They won't stand a chance."

Another burst rang out, and this time we heard the whine of ricochets. "That's a bit close," I remarked as we quickened our footsteps a little. "The Germans must have reached this end of town already. You don't think they're shooting at *us*?"

Eric shook his head. "Can't be. They wouldn't see us for the curve of the road. Just a couple of stray shots, I guess. Jerry must have reached this end of town and there's some sort of skirmish going on. We got out just in time if you ask me."

"Yes, and no thanks to that bloody half-colonel," I replied bitterly. "He just packed up and buggered off without bothering even to warn us, let alone take us with him."

Eric nodded assent as the rifle-fire began crackling again. "We'll give him a piece of our minds when we catch up with him!"

The firing died away as we got into the tight hairpin bends of the hill-slope. We plodded up the gradients as briskly as our inebriated condition would allow for twenty minutes or so, to be greeted eventually by half a dozen Maquisards who were acting as rearguard for the retreating main force.

We were amazed when they rushed towards us, smiling and waving their arms, then embraced us fervently as though we were a couple footballers who had just scored a goal.

"*Quel courage!*" they kept exclaiming, and gradually comprehension dawned on us. The rifle-fire Eric and I had heard as we retreated up the valley had not emanated from a street-skirmish in the town at all: it had been aimed at us by flank detachments of German troops advancing along the slopes of the valley as the main body entered the town by the road. The 'bravery' Eric and I had displayed in coolly continuing our unflurried retreat amid the hail of fire had thrown the Maquis into paroxysms of admiration. We refrained from pointing out that the 'hail of fire' had come from so far off that little of it came anywhere near us and that our 'bravery' was due to a combination of sheer ignorance and drink, not necessarily in that order. Had we understood that the bullets were aimed at us, the only thing to admire would have been the speed of our sprinting! Naturally we didn't explain this to the French but quickly assumed a modest demeanour, repeated a few times "Oh-anybody-else-would-have-done-the-same," and enjoyed our hour of glory so much that we almost forgot our anger at having been abandoned in the evacuation.

In any case it was the colonel we were cross with, not the French. He was responsible for us; they weren't. Their haste and confusion were understandable. They had miscalculated the speed of the German advance and driven straight into an ambush long before reaching their intended point of deployment. Several had been killed and a good many wounded before they could extricate themselves. Irregular troops defeated in a pitched battle could hardly be expected to conduct an orderly retreat and it was not to be wondered at that the occupants of the lorries had had no attention to spare for Eric and me.

With the colonel matters were different. He had not been involved in the battle; he was a regular soldier who should have been ready for emergencies; and as an officer of our own forces he ought to have looked to our safety as well as that of his team.

We told him so in forceful terms when we met him again a few minutes later. The liaison team were resting by the roadside and taking stock of their position in consultation with one or two of the Maquis leaders. They knew the Germans were bound to evacuate the town eventually, because they would not be able to spare the troops to hold it: this was the weakness of the whole German position in France. There was no knowing how long it would be before they departed, however. Moreover there were the Vichy authorities to take into account as well: they would certainly have brought in their own forces in the wake of the Germans, and these might stay indefinitely. Meanwhile, the scouts put out by the Maquis reported not only that the occupying force was getting stronger by the minute but that lorries and troops – including *milice* – were assembling with the obvious intention of pursuing us up the mountain road. It was clear we would have to take to the hilltops. The only question was when, if ever, it would be safe to come down again.

It didn't take long to decide that our best bet was to shift base permanently, and with this in view we set off on an all-night hike. Five days of gracious living had been insufficient to soften us up, but even so, it was not a journey Eric and I greatly enjoyed. In the first place, it was marred by the hangovers we were already developing from our drinking session of the afternoon: we had been banking on getting a good night's sleep in our pension. Secondly, there was the problem of Ted's wireless equipment. This included a generator and a couple of great hefty batteries. When the colonel ordered us peremptorily to help carry this lot, Eric and I boiled over; we weren't in the Army, we said, we were RAF, and if the Army couldn't be bothered with us when they evacuated the town, we couldn't be bothered with the Army when it came to humping wireless equipment. In the end, of course, we conceded that Ted couldn't carry all the gear himself and that it would be wrong to abandon it, but we insisted that the two Free French lieutenants should do their share as well, otherwise we wouldn't touch it. Even taking turns was bad enough, and by the time dawn broke we were all pretty much on our benders. It was mid-afternoon, however, before we reached the spot at which the Maquis had arranged for a car and driver to rendez-vous with us.

An hour or two later we arrived at our new head-quarters – a big, rambling farmhouse next door to a church and about five miles outside the village of Vals, which was a mountain holiday resort quite similar to the one we had just left. In fact the farmhouse seems to have been the vicarage, because its other occupants were the priest and his sister. How all this had been arranged I have no idea, but no doubt the Maquis were responsible. Fortunately the colonel was quartered elsewhere, so we found it pleasant enough living with Captain Montgomery, Ted and the two Free French officers.

We hadn't been living in the house more than a few days before we received news from Algiers via Ted's wireless that our team was to receive reinforcements from a quarter we hadn't expected – the American OSS. A couple of US Army captains and seven or eight master-sergeants, all French-speaking, were parachuted in a night or two later.

From then on, everything was wonderful, for as always wherever Americans go, profusion followed in their wake. When our wireless appeals for new RAF uniforms to replace our tattered Todt outfits were ignored, the Americans kitted us out with American uniforms. As far as I could figure out from the chevrons, this made us either corporals or two-star generals, but nobody gave a toss, least of all the Americans.

It goes without saying that the money flowed like water, and so did the wine. We had tremendous booze-ups at the local café, the biggest of all being on 6th June 1944 when the news of the D-Day landings came through. All the Americans were there, plus Captain Montgomery (but not the lieutenant-colonel), Ted, Eric, myself and the two Free French lieutenants. What the latter were doing there I can't think, because I remember they were disgusted with the hilarity of the rest of us on a day when, as they pointed out, hundreds of Frenchmen were dying. I thought this was daft, because there were all sorts of people dying all over the place all through the war, and for that matter there still are today, and unless you happen to be on the spot where it's going on, not having a party isn't going to help any of them.

There was another evening when we took Ted out boozing. Now Ted wasn't a drinking man, but we got him stiff as a board. He was supposed to take the broadcasts at certain times, and blind drunk though he was Ted couldn't forget his sense of duty. Over and over again as we carried him back to the farmhouse he kept weeping and mumbling, "When he knows, he'll kill me."

However, there was no problem, because Eric was a trained wireless operator and took the message without difficulty. Captain Montgomery took it all in good part and had a laugh, the lieutenant-colonel wasn't there, and the Americans of course didn't give a monkey's.

I must confess that the drinking got rather out of hand during this period. Eric and I never touched French beer because it was too much like soda pop. The large quantities of wine we guzzled with our meals we didn't regard as drinking at all. What we called drinking was the hard stuff, *eau de vie*, of which our intake was prodigious. We began to regard it as cissy to dilute it with anything else; real men swilled it down straight. We got to know a farmer who lived nearby. He had his own still for making *eau de vie* and a son whom we never saw sober. He didn't often see us in that condition either.

One day I broke into a rash again, and although I maintained it was nothing more than my usual crop of heat-spots, I consented in the end to be taken to a doctor, a Pole who could speak a fair amount of English. In response to his questioning I admitted how much I had been drinking. He threw up his hands in horror and said, "If you keep on like that much longer you'll have no liver left!"

He gave me some tablets, and every morning about six o'clock the old priest's sister would wake me up and force me to take half a dozen of them with hot water. I used to think what a terrible war it was and how upset my mother would be if she knew of my sufferings.

Now if all this sounds as though it didn't have very much to do with defeating the enemy; indeed it hadn't. On the other hand I had learnt from my now very considerable experience of the strange duties that could fall to the lot of a sergeant air gunner in the Royal Air Force that you could never tell what was going to happen next, so you might as well enjoy whatever there was to enjoy while it was still there.

It was probably just as well for my liver, however, that more serious business eventually began to obtrude itself upon our attention. D-Day had come and gone, and the rumours now were of further landings to take place in the south of France. Credit where credit is due: the Anglo-American team was working hard as well as playing hard, and for that matter I would not want to give the impression that Eric and I were idle apart from our elbow-lifting. There was always some way of making ourselves useful during the working day – carrying messages, giving a hand with domestic chores, servicing weapons, humping equipment about and so on.

The weapons and equipment, in fact, were increasing in quantity and range all the time. Arms drops from England and North Africa still continued after D-Day and after one of these we acquired two marvellous new possessions – a pair of bazookas. I took rather a fancy to these, and before long found myself trained as loader on one of them and teamed up with Brett, one of the American master-sergeants.

It wasn't long before we had an opportunity of trying out our new toy. One of the American captains approached Eric and me one day.

"Howja like to get into the war again, Norman?"

"All right," I replied. "What did you have in mind?"

"There's a couple of bridges over the river Rhône that the Maquis want us to blow. One's a suspension bridge where the highway goes over; the other's a railroad bridge. I'm scheduling the mission for tomorrow night. I figured on asking you to go with Brett on the suspension-bridge job. You guard the far side of the bridge with the bazooka while the charges are being laid. Any vehicles come along, you let them have it."

"Sounds a good scheme," I said.

The captain nodded. "OK. Full briefing tomorrow afternoon. Meantime you and Brett check your bazooka and see it's working." He turned to Eric. "How about you, Eric?"

"If Norman's going, I'll go," answered Eric. "You chaps have wined and dined us long enough: it's time we earned our keep."

"OK, great," said the captain. "You go with the second party and take care of the railroad bridge about a quarter of a mile away. Let's all see what a little Anglo-American cooperation can do."

So we got into the war again.

XII

Into the War Again

We set out the following evening just before midnight. Each team had an equal number of master-sergeants and was headed by an American captain. The rest of the force consisted of two lorry-loads of Maquis armed with a fearsome collection of Sten guns, rifles, revolvers and hand grenades. For my own part I had a Colt 45 – a terrifying weapon with a kick like a centre-forward's – and a commando knife strapped to my leg. It was thought possible I might have to use these even though my real business was with the bazooka.

We had been warned that the Germans were guarding the bridge so the first necessity was therefore to overpower the sentries. We couldn't hope to do this in silence, indeed, the clattering of our lorry would be enough to warn them of our arrival unless we were prepared to deploy a mile or two short of the objective – and this was out of the question because too many things could have gone wrong in the darkness. So we would have to rush them.

It went like clockwork. After driving for about an hour through the darkness the railroad-bridge party peeled off. A few minutes later our lorry roared up to the road-bridge at top speed and skidded to a halt. The Maquis boys leapt over the tailgate and ran like hell for the bridge. Not a sign of resistance revealed itself: there was nobody there.

Brett turned to me and grinned. "Well, Norm, whaddya know? No Krauts. Looks like we got a lousy intelligence service."

"I'm not complaining," said I.

"Nope, me neither. This is going to be a pushover."

"Let's not talk about pushovers until we're back in a safe warm bed."

But it was a pushover. In a couple of minutes we had the bazooka in position on the far side of the bridge. Brett and I settled ourselves comfortably in the roadway with a good field of fire. A couple of Maquisards placed themselves alongside us with a machine-gun, and two more men with carbines kept an eye on the flanks.

For twenty minutes or so we peered nervously into the blackness while the explosives party, consisting of three American NCOs covered by a group of Maquis, beavered away at the bridge supports down below. A kind of clanking noise in the distance gave us a fright at one point. We thought it might be a tank, but then it faded to nothingness again. Shortly afterwards one of the Frenchmen brought us word that the job was finished and the fuses were ready to be fired. We piled back into the lorries and drove off. A few minutes later we heard the explosion. A second explosion following within a minute of the first told us that the second party must have been successful too.

That seemed to be that, and Brett and I sat on our haunches on the floor of the lorry, smoking and chatting. The other American NCOs were doing the same. None of us was prepared for what happened as we passed through a small town. The lorry stopped without warning outside a house. At once the Maquis jumped to their feet and blazed away at it for a couple of minutes with everything they had – Stens, rifles, revolvers, the lot. The din was fearful. The flashes of the explosions illuminated the Americans' faces through the smoke, and I could see they were as horrified as I was. One of them jumped up and shook the shoulder of the nearest Frenchman.

"What in hell's going on?" he yelled. "What are you doing this for?"

The Frenchman's face gleamed with sweat. I'd heard of 'blood lust' but now I saw it for real. He waved a fist wildly.

"The family in that house, they have two sons in the Vichy *milice*," he bawled. "Two pig-sons in the *milice*!" He turned away and fired another burst at the windows from his tommy gun.

At last the firing died. The shouting and cursing stopped. From the house there was no sound. The driver banged the lorry into gear and we drove away. Behind us we left the stink of cordite, a litter of spent cartridges, and the pockmarked shell of what had been somebody's home.

When we got back to base, Brett and I discovered we'd taken the wrong mark of bazooka ammunition with us. If anything had come along the road towards the bridge we couldn't have fired a shot. We didn't let on to anybody…

During the ten or eleven months I spent with the Maquis, I didn't reflect much on how my personal adventures were related to the overall development of the war. It would have been a pretty hopeless speculation anyway. One day seemed much like another at the time, except for occasional bursts of activity or changes of environment. But the passage of time has telescoped my recollections and I see now that the French civil war fell into fairly well-defined stages. In the winter of 1943-44 the Maquis were forming into units, collecting arms and preparing for action. Sporadic raids and acts of sabotage – which were essentially directed at least as much against the Vichy government as against the Germans – accelerated into a regular campaign in the spring. The combined German-Vichy attack on the Alpine town in which Eric and I were holed up with the British liaison team marks the flare-up into out-and-out war. Our OSS-led operation against the bridge across the Rhone was part of the general Maquis offensive that started just before D-Day and continued through the period of high summer. By August the fruit was ripe for plucking. The Vichy régime had virtually ceased to hold any authority and it only remained to get rid of the Germans.

The Allied landings in the south of France took place on 15 August 1944. It had always been self-evident that the Germans lacked the numbers to put up more than a token resistance, so it didn't surprise us when the word came through that they were pulling out. Our job now was to harass the retreating Germans from the flanks. This we were very capable of doing, because the Maquis unit we were helping had grown to a strength of something like fifty or sixty Frenchmen, all living in the woods and deserted farmhouses round about. We had now received a couple of anti-tank guns in an arms drop. We also had a couple of Citroens that we had acquired from somewhere or other – bought with the almighty dollar, I expect – and by welding up a few odd bits of mild steel and scrap iron we produced a rig for towing the guns. So the Maquis had begun to resemble, within limits, a proper army. Essentially they were still, of course, groups of partisans conducting irregular warfare with small arms, but through the control exercised by the OSS and Allied teams parachuted into France and coordinated from London, they could be formed temporarily into larger units for specific tasks. On these occasions, supplemented by the American- and British-manned bazookas and light artillery now available, they constituted a formidable fighting force.

They had even begun to acquire a bit of a 'tail' in the shape of camp-followers of various kinds. Not all of those who were now straggling in to join them really wanted to fight for the liberation of France. Many regarded the Maquis merely as a refuge against some worse fate. Some were very likely ex-collaborators jumping on the Gaullist bandwagon while there was still time. Others were young Frenchmen who had been conscripted into the now disintegrating Todt organisation. Yet others were Todt workers of Soviet origin with a complex past and a gloomy future. Having surrendered as Soviet soldiers at Stalingrad in breach of orders to fight to the last man, they now feared to be repatriated in case of being shot for cowardice.

There were two roads leading north along which the German columns would have to retire. Our main force accordingly went to the major of these roads, taking the two anti-tank guns, one of the bazookas and all the Anglo-Americans except Brett and me. We and our bazooka were attached to the smaller force, consisting of about twenty-five Frenchmen, whose task was to harass the Germans using the minor road. We marched across country for a day or two, sleeping rough, and finally found ourselves on a hilltop overlooking the road. A small river flowed through the valley between us and the road, but at one point a bridge carried the road over the river to our side. Two things were plain at a glance. Firstly, we could snipe at passing troops from the hillside and be in reasonable safety though from some distance away. Secondly, if we destroyed the bridge we could block the traffic, get in close and then really give them a bad time.

The trouble was the Germans had thought it all out before us. We couldn't get near the bridge because on the near side of it was an isolated house, and according to a local civilian whom we had encountered there was a German machine-gun nest in it. There wasn't a shred of cover from which to attack the house anywhere on our side.

The French fumed and chattered away with frustration. Finally they approached Brett and me.

"We have to take that house," said the Maquis leader.

"You'll never do it," answered Brett.

"But we have to. If we take the house we can blow the bridge, then the Boches who come along the road are kaput."

"How can you do it? There isn't a scrap of cover. They'll mow you all down before you get within a hundred yards. They'll have machine guns at every window. What you need is artillery, and you haven't got any. Our anti-tank guns are with the main force."

"All right then. What about the bazooka? Your rockets will go through the walls of the house, won't they?"

"They might, but not from here. To get a good shot we've got to be a lot closer than this."

"Get closer then!"

"Not me, pal." Brett sighed patiently. "Look, there's five hundred yards of open ground in front of that house. You want Norman and me to carry this thing half that distance, then stand still with it balanced on my shoulder and poop it off at that fortress? What do you think the Krauts will be doing all that time? How many shots do you think it'll take to knock them out? And how many rounds d'you figure we'll get off before they blow our asses off, even supposing they ever let us reach our firing position?"

"But at night then?"

Brett shook his head decisively. "No sir. No different. Not a chance. Not at night, not any time. I don't aim to commit suicide, not in this war I don't. What do you say, Norm?"

"I'm on your side. I don't fancy it one little bit."

"So what are we to do?" asked the Frenchman impatiently.

"Do? I'll tell you what you do," said Brett. "You keep up here on the hill during the day. At night you move down as near the road as you dare, keeping yourselves well spread out, well clear of that goddamn house and well in line for a fast sprint back up the hill if there's any trouble. When the Krauts come along the road you can pick 'em off as best you can. Me and Norm'll stand by to take care of any trucks or half-tracks."

"We'll only be able to kill a few of them that way."

"Jeez, get a load of him!" exclaimed Brett. "Yeah, well, they'll only be able to kill a few of you too, maybe none if you keep your eyes skinned – have you thought of that? What do you want, a goddam massacre?"

"Yes," replied the Frenchman viciously, and turned on his heel.

We watched him walk back to the other Maquisards. As they resumed their deliberations, Brett tapped his finger slowly against the side of his head. "You know what them stupid bastards are gonna decide, Norm? They're gonna belly-crawl down to that house tonight and when they get to their feet to run the last fifty yards the Krauts'll blast 'em into little pieces. And where's little ole Brett and little ole Norman gonna be? Up here where it's good an' safe, that's where, right?"

"Too bloody right!" I said.

It turned out just as Brett had predicted. The French crept down, rushed the house and got the massacre they wanted, if not in the way they wanted it. It was all over in a few minutes. Brett and I stayed at the top of the hill listening to the firing and yelling – mostly Germans firing and Frenchmen yelling. Then the assault party trickled silently back. They had taken a lot of casualties – just how many we never knew, because they moved them out fast.

But next morning we did see one of the wounded who had died during the night. He had been hit in the stomach, we thought by a dum-dum bullet because the hole in his back where the bullet had come out was big enough to put your fist in. His knees were doubled up in agony, and the palms of his hands were covered with blood where his fingernails had dug into them. The French were very upset about him, and even I, in my unimaginative way, found the sight unappetising.

Brett and I kept quiet. There was no point in saying "I told you so." But we thought it.

Next night we did things Brett's way. Taking care to keep out of range of the fortified house, we came part-way down the slope and spread ourselves along walls and behind trees overlooking the road. Sure enough, as soon as darkness came to offer protection against Allied aircraft, which now prevented all movement on French roads and railways during the day, the Germans began to appear, in groups or singly, some walking, some on bicycles or in farm carts pulled by horses. It was a pretty confused business, because the range was maybe three hundred yards or more and the targets were indistinct in the dark, but we blazed away with rifles, tommy guns and Brens at every movement we spotted, while the Germans returned our fire as best they could. The battle flared up and died away at intervals during the night. We had all the advantages on our side – height, cover and the simple fact that the enemy's aim was to proceed along the road and ours wasn't. There was no question of our being able to prevent all of them, or even most of them, from getting through, but we must have given them a miserable time and I have no doubt that we caused a good few casualties. As for ourselves, there were plenty of bullets whistling and pinging around our ears, but disregarding the disastrous attack on the German-occupied house I don't think we took a single casualty.

We kept it up like this for three or four nights and were just beginning to get accustomed to the routine when one night no more targets presented themselves on the road. We approached as near as we dared to the fortified house, which had supported the troops on the road during the night battles with its machine-gun fire. We fired a few rounds towards it without provoking any reply. Next morning a group of volunteers went down and investigated the house. The Germans had pulled out. The last of the retiring columns must now be clear.

This was the signal for us to move off to another location where, according to the Maquis intelligence sources, there were other German troops in retreat. God knows what distance we covered, because we force-marched, but of course our state of fitness was such that it meant nothing to us. Sleeping rough was no hardship either: the nights were warm, and it was quiet and peaceful under the stars.

One problem that did trouble us on this march, however, was shortage of food. We were living on nothing much more than grapes and wine. During the three or four days when we were harassing the retreating German forces from the hillside, as a matter of fact, I was as weak as a kitten from dysentery brought on by drinking wine that had gone sour. Brett and the French all kidded me that the only thing wrong with me was drinking too much of it, but quite seriously the trouble was that we had nowhere to store the stuff and it went off through standing in the sun.

Another incident arising from the shortage of food produced a good illustration of the tensions beneath the French political surface. We happened at the time to be crossing a sector in which a communist Maquis group was operating. We actually passed by the farmhouse that served as their headquarters, and spoke to some of them. They were quite friendly towards Brett and me, and gave us food without hesitation. But they flatly refused to give any to their compatriots of our group, whom they regarded with barely-veiled hostility. It was sad to witness such a scene at a time when the need for unity among Frenchmen was so self-evident.

Of course, as I've said before, the communists aimed to take over France themselves after the liberation, and in these last stages of the German occupation it looked as though they might well succeed. They got a lot of their strength by cashing in on the bitterness that followed the French capitulation of 1940. The collaborationist régime was of the right wing: the communists, on the other hand, were uncompromising apostles of resistance – at any rate after June 1941 when the Germans invaded Russia. In addition, many French Catholics swung right over to atheistic communism during the occupation in disgust at the attitude of the Church. Rightly or wrongly, they suspected the Church of being more concerned with preserving its own privileges than with the sufferings of its flock or with resisting evil as personified by Hitler. Claude, my French friend in my first Maquis group, told me that his widowed mother lived in Clermont Ferrand, where food shortages were very severe at times. Despite all the hardships, however, the priests continued to call once a week as they were accustomed to do, expecting the usual cheese, milk, eggs and so forth to be available for collection. Claude was consequently most bitter against the Church, and although he himself did not turn communist, there were many others in his sort of situation who did.

We moved on, and the French managed to scrounge food from somewhere or other. It was around this stage of our march that we picked up a couple of German prisoners. I didn't myself happen to see them come in, but apparently they walked straight up the road to meet us. They were in uniforms but without arms, and they made no attempt at resistance. We had no means of imprisoning them, so all we could do was take them along with us. We could keep only the loosest kind of guard on them: it consisted mainly of seeing that they didn't get the chance to make a snatch at any of our weapons.

Any such intention seemed far from their minds, however. On the contrary, they appeared glad to be able to tag along and be fed and watered. Their boots were worn out and one of them had feet that were covered in blood from broken blisters. What did seem to upset them was the discovery that I was British, though they were friendly enough towards Brett. I asked them why.

"I think you know why," replied one of them coldly.

"No, I don't. Tell me," I replied.

"Because of what you British do to prisoners."

"Eh?" I was nonplussed. "What do you mean? What do we do to prisoners then?"

"You shoot them."

"Rubbish!" I scoffed. "Of course we don't shoot them."

"It is true. You do not respect the Geneva Convention."

I tried to argue with him, but it was no use. According to him, the German troops in France all believed that as a form of revenge for the manacling of British prisoners after the Dieppe raid, the British didn't take prisoners. I know now, as I had no means of knowing then, that in the heat of the events just after D-Day there were instances of Canadian troops (who had suffered heavily at Dieppe) shooting German prisoners, just as there had been one or two notorious shootings of British prisoners by the Germans in the Dunkirk campaign of 1940. Such happenings were not typical on either side, but perhaps these two had heard rumours generated by them: at any rate, nothing I could say would convince them that I was harmless, and soon I gave up trying. After all, it didn't matter two hoots to me whether they were frightened of me or not.

We reached our new position in good time and set up our ambush. The road on which the retreating German column was expected passed at this point between an almost sheer cliff on one side and a grassy hill-slope on the other.

Our plan was simple. The Maquis had by this time a fairly clear idea of the German technique of retirement.

The best troops were in Russia, of course, and those stationed in France were a bit of a rag-tag lot, made up of Nazi collaborators and other oddments from all the countries of Occupied Europe; a good number were even Ukrainians or Mongolians taken prisoner on the Eastern Front. However, each retreating column would have a hard core of German troops assigned to it, and these would form the advance party, with a half-track or tank if available. Brett and I, therefore, had the job of dealing with the latter by means of our bazooka.

We placed ourselves in a hollow on the hillside, about fifty yards or so from the road. A party of about twenty Maquis distributed themselves around us among the plentiful boulders and bushes. While we were dealing with the armour they were to pour in covering fire from their rifles and light machine-guns. The remainder of our force, about five men, were positioned on top of the cliff opposite; they were to bombard the Germans with hand grenades. It was to be a hit-and-run affair, of course, and we would head for the tall timber as soon as the opposition became serious.

It would have been a good plan if it had worked properly.

We slept in our battle positions. The French were standing guard and were supposed to wake us up when they heard the German column approaching. The Germans must have been moving very quietly, however, or else (which seems more likely) our sentries had gone to sleep, because suddenly Brett was shaking my shoulder violently and hissing, "Get off your ass, Norm, the goddam Krauts are here!"

It was dawn. Dew and a sluggish-looking mist lay on the grass. The steam-rollering sound of a half-track in the not very far distance galvanised me into life. Brett got the bazooka balanced on his shoulder and I slammed a rocket into it before the sleep was out of my eyes. We were none too soon, because at that precise instant the half-track appeared around the bend a hundred and fifty yards away, with a column of troops marching behind.

Brett fired, and the rocket hit the road just in front of the half-track and ricocheted into it. The Germans must have been first-class troops, because they got organised in no time at all. Even as I was reloading for our second shot I saw one burly chap – he must have been an RSM or something – standing in the open giving orders as cool as a cucumber. He'd got men deployed and firing in our direction by the time Brett got his second shot away. This one smashed straight into the half-track, which went up at once in a sheet of flame. I heard the screaming of its occupants above the rattle of small-arms fire.

At this instant the French covering party broke and ran, one of them shouting to me that there were Germans advancing along the hillside and among the trees above our own positions. We didn't stop to enquire how they had got there – and in any case our job was already done – we just grabbed the bazooka and our spare rockets and joined the flight uphill. As we did so an intermittent coughing noise made itself heard through the crackle of rifles and Schmeissers: the Germans had managed to get a mortar or two into action in record time. The shells burst among us one after the other, flinging clods of earth and splinters of rock in all directions, but not surprisingly the aim was wild.

We soon reached the shelter of the trees – where I ran almost into the arms of a German soldier. I don't know which of us was more surprised. I didn't stop to discuss the point but legged it straight past him as hard as I could go. He didn't fire a single shot after me. I imagine he was as terrified as I was.

We re-formed and counted heads as soon as we had got a safe distance away in the hills. Somewhat to our surprise, we found we had lost none of our numbers. Even more astonishing, our two prisoners straggled in and joined up with us again: we had of course abandoned them down by the road during the brief battle. They were still in their German uniforms and could certainly have returned to their fellow-countrymen in the confusion had they wanted to, but I suppose they felt they were well out of the war and didn't want to get involved again.

When I think of all the stuff Brett and I were carrying and the distance we had to cover uphill I feel we were very lucky to escape. Just about everything had gone wrong. Not only had our sentries fallen asleep, the Germans had had an advance party of infantry sweeping the hillsides for ambushers ahead of the half-track. The half-track had been following a little too closely behind the advance party, however, and this had just given us sufficient time to destroy it before we were flushed. I don't believe our group on the cliff opposite got a single grenade off at the Germans: perhaps Brett and I had stopped the half-track before the troop-column came within throwing range. Summing up, both from our point of view and from the

Germans' too, it all went to show that in military operations the world over, Murphy's law applies: *if anything can go wrong, it will.*

That night we crossed the road – a little nervously, in case we encountered any German traffic – and rejoined the main Maquis force next day. I found Eric and compared notes with him. His group had laid an ambush for a larger German column retreating on the main road, and they also had been involved in quite a pantomime.

"It was broad daylight before they appeared," said Eric, "so we had a good view. Our anti-tank guns were sited up on the hillside and the French with their small arms were spread out below and in front of us, so we were firing over their heads.

"The Germans were using all kinds of transport. There were horse-drawn carts, bicycles, a lorry or two, that sort of stuff. We waited until they'd got their heads well into the noose, then we started shooting. It was a piece of duff really, just like target practice. We smashed up two or three horse-drawn carts and knocked men down like ninepins. In the meantime the French were giving it to them with rifles and Brens. It was a right shambles: bodies lying about all over the place, carts and lorries piling into each other, and a lot of shouting and screaming going on.

"We did pretty well, I reckon. We must have got half a dozen rounds into them from each of our anti-tank guns before they got sorted out and started coming after us.

"Groups of them formed together, with officers and NCOs waving and blowing whistles, then they came up the hillside in line abreast just like on a parade ground. If we'd had a couple of heavy machine-guns we could have murdered them. But of course we hadn't, so there was no point in hanging about and we beat it as fast as we could go. We had to abandon the guns of course, but the funny thing was that we came back in the afternoon and collected them again, and they were completely undamaged. The Germans hadn't even slashed the tyres. With it being well on into the morning I expect they wanted to get on in case of being caught by Allied aircraft."

This was very likely so. By this time, the mastery achieved by the British and American air forces was so complete that virtually nothing moved on French roads by daylight. Even the Maquis didn't dare to drive about unless the roof of the vehicle was marked with a large star.

I told Eric of my own experiences with the smaller group. He lit a cigarette when I had finished my recital.

"That was a narrow squeak you had with the German soldier," he remarked.

"The whole bloody do was a narrow squeak!" I replied.

We were both silent for a moment or two before Eric spoke again.

"Norman?"

"What?"

"Are you thinking what I'm thinking?"

"What are you thinking?"

"I'm wondering how much more of this we ought to do – going out on these shoot-ups, I mean. We've always said we're evaders, not soldiers."

"Well, I don't know really. I suppose we've just sort of drifted into it, haven't we? But we couldn't just have sat on our arses waiting for liberation, not once everybody else had started fighting."

"Right enough. But do you think liberation's all that far away? We'd look a bit stupid after all we've been through if we got ourselves killed at the last minute on one of these guerrilla larks."

"You've got a point," I said. "Perhaps we ought to pack it in. Anyhow let's see what the news is when we get back to base."

The news was like music to our ears. Ted had got it over his wireless that the Allied invasion forces were within 24 hours of where we were. That was enough for Eric and me. No more operations.

Perhaps this was a pity, because next day we missed the most spectacularly successful operation that our Maquis unit was involved in. They were out in force, with the bazookas, anti-tank guns and everything, headed by the American OSS group. Brett told us later what happened.

"We wuz spread out over this hillside overlooking the road, all set to make plenty trouble for the Krauts. Pretty soon this column of soldiers appears, an' they look a bit of a mess. They got the usual crappy collection of farm carts and bicycles, but there's no half-tracks or armour, an' they don't even have a proper advance-guard out. There musta been four, five hundred of 'em.

"Well, the boys are just gettin' their weapons cocked ready to let 'em have it when they get into range, but at this point the cap'n passes the word to hold fire. Then he gets up, waves at the Krauts and marches straight down the middle of the road towards 'em, keepin' his tommy gun slung over his shoulder out of the way.

"Some Kraut officer halts the column an' comes to the front to meet the cap'n, an' they salute one another just like on parade, an' the cap'n he says we're part of the invasion forces an' we've by-passed the Germans, an' they better surrender pronto or we're gonna clobber 'em.

"Well, some of us begin to show ourselves a teensy bit, just to show the cap'n ain't shittin' sheep-pellets, an' of course the Krauts see our American uniforms an' they don't know we're only Maquis. The talkin' goes on a minute or two an' some of the Krauts start gettin' restless, an' for that matter so do we.

"Then whaddya think happens? A goddam tank appears way down the highway comin' from behind the Germans, an' it ain't one of theirs – it's an advance unit of the real invasion force lookin' for trouble.

"So that's enough for the Kraut commander. He orders his men to put their weapons down an' surrender, an' we come down an' pick 'em up, an' gee, does he look sick when he finds we're just a bunch of guerrillas an' not regular troops after all!

"But by this time it's too late, o' course, an' anyways he couldn't have done much with this lousy crew he's got: only the officers an' non-coms are Germans – the enlisted men are Mongolians an' God knows what all, an' none of 'em look like they aim to earn no Iron Crosses.

"So now we got 'em all prisoner, an' they're gonna be a goddam nuisance till we can dump 'em somewheres."

The prisoners were indeed an embarrassment. Eric and I went out and had a look at them. They were lolling about in the open under the eye of a few Maquis armed with tommy guns. They looked a feeble crowd, as Brett had said, but even so we wouldn't have been able to cope with them for long. We couldn't even have fed them. They were soon roused up and marched away, however. The Maquis took them into a town nearby, where I believe they were put into a factory compound that had been turned into a temporary POW camp.

I suppose this was just about the end of the war as far as Eric and I were concerned: our Maquis service didn't come to any very exciting conclusion but just fizzled out like a damp fuse. Our final liberation, too, was marked by no great moment of climax: it happened in dribbles.

The day after the prisoners went we got the news that French liberation troops had entered Vals. All the Maquis went down to celebrate. Eric and I felt it was their celebration, however, and we should leave them to it, so we stayed where we were, in the Anglo-American farmhouse where we were still living.

After that things began to move. Captain Montgomery arranged for us to be taken south a day or so later by a car with a Maquis driver. It didn't take us long to get ready: we had no more possessions now than when we'd been shot down. We emptied a final bottle or two with the lads, shook hands with Ted and Captain Montgomery and all the OSS Americans who'd looked after us so well. Then we were away.

We got on to the N7 and headed straight down to Avignon. By this time the German troops had all gone, but the roads and ditches were littered with their débris – tanks, lorries, guns and equipment of every kind, some shot-up or burnt-out, some just abandoned. As we approached Avignon we hit streams of northward-moving Allied military traffic. We drove through the town without difficulty, but the famous bridge had an RAF-type hole in the middle, and we were held up a long time before we were allowed across the single-file pontoon that was temporarily replacing it.

It was just the other side of Avignon that we saw our first RAF unit. It was a radio truck pulled in at the side of the road. We stopped, got out of the car and asked one of the airmen standing by the truck to fetch his officer.

A flight lieutenant appeared at the door. "Yes, what can I do for you?" he enquired.

I pointed down at my American corporal's uniform and assumed my broadest Yorkshire accent.

"You might not think so from t'luke of us," I said, "but we're shot-down British aircrew. We've been tryin' to get home for t'last twelve moonth."

The flight lieutenant looked startled. "Oh, I see," he said, and paused awkwardly, clearly unsure what to do next. Then natural good manners came to the fore as a bright idea struck him. "Well, I expect you could do with a cup of tea after your journey?"

Eric and I looked at each other.

"By gum, we could that," I said.

POSTSCRIPT

The officer in charge of the radio truck directed Norman Lee and Eric Brearley to an American-operated airfield nearby. Next day they were flown to Naples. At a transit camp there they were kitted out with British uniforms, supplied with a small sum of pay, and cheated of their beer ration by a swindling sergeant-major. They were next transported to Casablanca to take their places on the roster for an aircraft to England. A final fling on cheap vino, financed by money they had talked the well-meaning CO of a nearby RAF detachment into providing from his welfare funds, culminated in the arrival of a jeep-load of 'snowdrops' (American military police) and a brief taste of the delights of an American military 'cooler'.

Aboard a homeward-bound aircraft at last, they were ejected just before takeoff in favour of two German prisoners, who had a higher priority. On hearing their story, a Royal Air Force flight lieutenant gave up his seat for Eric, but a squadron leader padre refused to do the same for Norman.

Thus Norman arrived in England a day after Eric. After participating in one of those scenes, notorious during the war, in which unbending customs officers subjected homecoming fighting men to rigorous search in the hope of mulcting them for large sums in import duty, he was locked into a London-bound railway carriage with four other returning evaders. The aim of this imprisonment was to prevent members of the public from speaking to them before they had been interrogated. On reaching London, however, they were at large on the railway station for two hours before a Service car arrived to take them to the Air Ministry.

After interrogation, Norman and his four companions were sent for medical examination. They went into a quick huddle and agreed that, having survived the war safely thus far they were not going to risk their necks by flying again when the war was almost won. So they all deliberately failed the test in which mercury has to be blown up a glass tube and held at a certain level.

The president of the medical board emerged from his office shortly afterwards and announced, "You're a shower of bloody malingerers! If you think you're getting off flying this way you're bloody well mistaken, because I'm certifying you all bloody well fit!"

They all laughed heartily at this and admitted they were as fit as fleas. Nevertheless, before Norman departed the medical officer handed him a chit for 28 days' sick leave on the vague ground that he could probably do with some time off. With this added to his 28 days survivor's leave, there was plenty of time to savour again the pleasure of home life, and for the first fortnight Norman scarcely set foot outside the house.

Later on he visited Eric Brearley and his wife at their home in Southport, and one day the three of them amused themselves by going to the Post Office together to draw Mrs Brearley's widow's pension, which had not yet been stopped. (Although the Air Ministry had soon got to know that Eric and Norman were in France, they had allowed their respective families to continue believing they were dead as a precaution against the enemy's discovering their whereabouts.)

For the next few months Norman was posted from one holding unit to another. After VE Day he applied to remain in the Royal Air Force and served as an air gunner on Lincolns and Lancasters until 1949. By this time the requirement for air gunners was disappearing with the introduction of new types of aircraft and new forms of air combat.

Leaving the Royal Air Force, Norman sampled civilian life as a baker in Shipley, Yorkshire, for a few years, but found he did not like it much.

He rejoined the Royal Air Force in 1952 for a full career in an administrative capacity, and from then until final retirement as a warrant officer his work rarely took him anywhere near aeroplanes. The spectacular wine-drinking of his Maquis days was not continued or repeated in later life. Neither did he ever revisit the south of France. But he did marry, lived happily ever after and had two children, now grown up. He still takes life as it comes, does not worry, and claims to have no imagination. He says that if called upon to do so, he would cheerfully fight his war all over again.

APPENDIX

Operations Flown By Sergeant Norman Lee on Active Service with RAF Bomber Command, 1943

The source for most of the details of Bomber Command operations given below is the admirably comprehensive reference work *The Bomber Command War Diaries 1939-1945* by Martin Middlebrook and Chris Everitt.

2/3 AUGUST 1943, HAMBURG

Force despatched: 329 Lancasters, 235 Halifaxes, 105 Stirlings, 60 Wellingtons, 5 Mosquitoes = 740 total

Losses: 13 Lancasters, 10 Halifaxes, 4 Wellingtons, 3 Stirlings = 30 (4.1%)

This was the last attack of the 'Battle of Hamburg' which had included the notorious 'firestorm' and wiped out vast areas of the city. Nevertheless this final raid was not successful. Many aircraft turned back because of extensive thunderstorms over Germany. Others bombed alternative targets. Some aircraft losses were caused by weather. Bombing at Hamburg was sporadic.

9/10 AUGUST 1943, MANNHEIM

Force despatched: 286 Lancasters, 171 Halifaxes = 457 total.

Losses: 3 Lancasters, 6 Halifaxes = 9 (2%)

Cloud over the target area caused bombing to be scattered. 1316 buildings were destroyed or severely damaged according to the exceptionally detailed German reports. 42 industrial firms lost production. Casualties were 269 killed, 1210 injured. 1528 fires were caused. 8 railway locomotives, 146 passenger carriages and 40 goods wagons were damaged or destroyed.

10/11 AUGUST 1943, NUREMBERG

Force despatched: 318 Lancasters, 216 Halifaxes, 119 Stirlings = 653 total

Losses: 6 Lancasters, 7 Halifaxes, 3 Stirlings = 16 (2.5%)

Pathfinder markers obscured by cloud, but central and south Nuremberg were heavily hit, and an extensive 'fire area' developed. 577 persons were reported killed.

12/13 AUGUST 1943, MILAN

Force despatched: 321 Lancasters, 183 Halifaxes = 504 total

Losses: 1 Lancaster, 2 Halifaxes = 3 (0.6%)

This raid was part of a general bomber offensive against Italy ordered at political level to encourage Italy's exit from the war. (Italy surrendered on 8 September.) The raid was considered successful and probably caused most of the damage and casualties reported in Milan during August, including severe damage to 4 major factories (one of them the Alfa Romeo works), the main railway station and the La Scala opera house.

17/18 AUGUST 1943, PEENEMUNDE

Force despatched: 324 Lancasters, 218 Halifaxes, 54 Stirlings = 596 aircraft

Losses: 23 Lancasters, 15 Halifaxes, 2 Stirlings = 40 (6.7%)

A difficult and hazardous operation against a priority target. The high percentage loss of attacking aircraft reflects this. (Peenemunde was the research establishment on the Baltic coast where V-2 rockets were being developed and tested.) Special features of the raid were:

a) This was a 'precision' raid against a small target, not an 'area' raid

b) A moonlit night was selected, despite the advantage this gave the defenders, to help the accuracy of bombing

c) This was the first occasion on which the raid was controlled over the target by a 'Master Bomber' (Group Captain Searsby of 83 Sqn, 11 Group)

d) A Mosquito 'diversion' raid on Berlin drew off the night fighters during the first two waves of the attack. (Norman Lee was in the third wave, by which time the defences were functioning at full strength, as reflected by the third-wave losses: 17 of 109 aircraft from 5 Group, 12 out of 57 aircraft from Canadian 6 Group.)

e) This was the first time the Germans used *schräge Musik* night-fighters. These were Me 110s with upward-firing cannon allowing them to approach and attack from below – the bombers' 'blind spot'.

1800 tons of bombs were dropped, and the V-2 attacks on Britain were set back by about 2 months as a result of the destruction caused.

22/23 AUGUST 1943, LEVERKUSEN

Force despatched: 257 Lancasters, 192 Halifaxes, 13 Mosquitoes = 462 aircraft

Losses: 3 Lancasters, 2 Halifaxes = 5 (1.1%)

Thick cloud over the target and partial failure of 'Oboe' navigation signals caused dispersal of effort. Only a few bombs fell on Leverkusen, causing some superficial damage to the IG Farben chemical plant. Other bombs fell on twelve different towns including Dusseldorf and Solingen.

23/24 AUGUST 1943, BERLIN

Force despatched: 335 Lancasters, 251 Halifaxes, 124 Stirlings, 17 Mosquitoes = 727 total

Losses: 17 Lancasters, 23 Halifaxes, 16 Stirlings = 56 [largest number lost on a single night so far in the war] (7.9%)

Despite the use of Mosquitoes to mark navigation points and a Master Bomber over the target, this raid was only partially successful. The markers were laid too far south, so that much of the attack fell outside the city. Even so it was Berlin's most serious raid yet, with 2611 buildings destroyed or damaged. Some bombs fell in the city centre, especially on government buildings in the Wilhelmstrasse. 20 vessels were sunk on the city's canals. 854 people were killed, including two POWs. The raid was the first of three, which were probably intended to open a 'Battle of Berlin' similar to that which had wiped out Hamburg. The overall results were disappointing, however. The high casualties reflect both the long distance to the target and the ferocity of the flak and fighter defences. Over the three raids, 125 aircraft were lost out of a total of 1669 sorties – a loss rate of 7.5%. The attempted 'Battle of Berlin' was abandoned for the time being.

5/6 SEPTEMBER 1943, MANNHEIM

Force despatched: 299 Lancasters, 195 Halifaxes, 111 Stirlings = 605 total

Losses: 13 Lancasters, 13 Halifaxes, 8 Stirlings = 34 (5.6%)

A successful raid, with excellent Pathfinder marking. The destruction caused was described as 'catastrophic' in official German reports.

6/7 SEPTEMBER 1943, MUNICH

Force despatched: 257 Lancasters, 147 Halifaxes = 404 total.

Losses: 3 Lancasters, 13 Halifaxes = 16 (4%)

City covered by cloud: hence marking hampered and not very effective. Bombing was mostly scattered over the south and west of the city.

15/16 SEPTEMBER 1943, MONTLUCON

Force despatched: 209 Halifaxes, 120 Stirlings, 40 Lancasters, 5 B-17s (American) = 369 total (excluding Americans)

Losses: 2 Halifaxes, 1 Stirling = 3 (0.8%)

A highly successful precision raid by moonlight on the Dunlop rubber factory. Accurate marking by Pathfinders, excellent Master Bomber control. All factory buildings hit. The American participation was part of a familiarisation and experimental programme by US bombing forces in Britain, which otherwise operated mainly by daylight and employed an entirely different offensive doctrine and technique.

16/17 SEPTEMBER 1943, MODANE

Force despatched: 170 Halifaxes, 127 Stirlings,, 43 Lancasters, 5 B-17s (American) = 340 total (excluding Americans)

Losses: 2 Halifaxes, 1 Stirling = 3 (0.9%)

An attack on important railway yards on the main route between France and Italy. Marking was unsuccessful and bombing accordingly inaccurate.

22/23 SEPTEMBER 1943, HANNOVER

Force despatched: 322 Lancasters, 226 Halifaxes, 137 Stirlings, 26 Wellingtons, 5 B-17s (American) = 711 total (excluding Americans)

Losses: 7 Lancasters, 12 Halifaxes, 5 Stirlings, 2 Wellingtons = 26 (3.7%)

Despite good visibility, strong winds caused inaccurate marking, with bombing consequently concentrated 2-5 miles south of the city centre.

Diversionary raids on Oldenburg and Emden by a total of 21 Lancasters and 20 Mosquitoes may have helped reduce casualties.

23/24 SEPTEMBER 1943, MANNHEIM

Force despatched: 312 Lancasters, 193 Halifaxes, 115 Stirlings, 8 Mosquitoes, 5 B-17s (American) = 628 total (excluding Americans)

Losses: 18 Lancasters, 7 Halifaxes, 7 Stirlings = 32 (5.1%)

This raid was intended to destroy the northern area of Mannheim, which had escaped in earlier raids. Marking was successful and bombing well concentrated. Many buildings were destroyed or damaged. 102 people were killed, 418 injured, 25,000 bombed out. Later stages of the bombing crept into Ludwigshafen, on the other side of the Rhine, where the IG Farben chemical plant was destroyed, 47 people killed, 260 injured and 8,000 bombed out.

A diversionary raid was mounted on Darmstadt by 21 Lancasters and 8 Mosquitoes.

UN GRAND BORDEL

29/30 SEPTEMBER 1943, BOCHUM

Force despatched: 213 Lancasters, 130 Halifaxes, 9 Mosquitoes = 352 total

Losses: 4 Lancasters, 5 Halifaxes = 9 (2.6%)

The Pathfinder plan worked excellently. Bombing was accurate and concentrated. The Old City suffered severely. 161 people were killed, including 33 foreign workers and POWs; 337 injured.

4/5 OCTOBER 1943, FRANKFURT

Force despatched: 162 Lancasters, 170 Halifaxes, 70 Stirlings, 4 Mosquitoes, 3 B-17s (American) = 406 total (excluding Americans)

Losses: 3 Lancasters, 5 Halifaxes, 2 Stirlings = 10 (2.5%)

Clear weather: good Pathfinder marking. Extensive destruction caused in the eastern half of the city and to the inland docks of the river Main. Many city centre buildings hit, new Rathaus (town hall) burnt out. A hit on an orphanage in a former Jewish hospital killed 90 children and 14 nuns and other staff. There was a considerable exodus from Frankfurt via the railway stations on the following days. (Norman Lee's aircraft was shot down before it reached the city. When two of its crew-members who had been captured were at Frankfurt station waiting to be taken to the POW processing centre, it is perhaps not surprising that their military escort had to protect them from being assaulted or worse by an irate crowd.)

A diversionary raid on Ludwigshafen was carried out by 66 Lancasters on this night.

SOME GENERAL COMMENTS

Norman Lee flew his seventeen operations with Bomber Command just after what can be regarded as a kind of 'halfway point' in the air war, when early lessons had been digested and the foundations of the subsequent Allied air superiority laid. Bomber Command's offensive against Germany had been hampered during the first three years (1939-42) by the fact that navigational techniques, aircraft performance, and above all the numbers of aircraft available, were simply inadequate for the job the Command was trying to do. Many raids had been total failures, and many relatively 'successful' ones caused far less real damage than was believed at the time.

During the first half of 1943, however, the Command was re-equipped with large numbers of 'second-generation' bomber types - four-engined Stirlings, Halifaxes and Lancasters with their superior performance and heavier payloads, along with fast twin-engined Mosquitoes for specialised tasks. It is illustrative of Bomber Command's offensive having just passed the 'halfway point' that Norman Lee's tour coincided with the last two or three occasions on which the twin-engined Wellington, generally considered the best of the earlier generation of RAF bombers, was used in front-line Bomber Command service (the Hampdens and Whitleys having already been phased out).

New doctrines and techniques were evolving, including the locating and marking of targets by 'Pathfinders' and the swamping of the defences by faster and more concentrated delivery of bombloads over the target areas. New electronic and radio devices radically improved navigation and in the end over-mastered the enemy's counter-electronic measures. In this respect Norman Lee's tour was concurrent with numerous important innovations: the first use, during the Battle of Hamburg, of 'window' (vast quantities of aluminium foil strips) to confuse enemy radar, which rendered the German night-fighter control system obsolete at a stroke; well-organised subsidiary raids against towns far from the main target to decoy German night-fighters and railway-mounted flak guns away from the main target; the Master Bomber circling over the target area and controlling the attacking force.

None of this meant that the German defenders stood still. Skilful fighter control, radar-directed master searchlights and flak gunnery, along with such innovations as the *schräge Musik* night-fighter technique, took a heavy toll of the attackers. The supremacy ultimately achieved by Bomber Command (operating mainly at night) in conjunction with the US Eighth Air Force (mainly by day) came about neither easily nor suddenly. Thus the spectacular success of some of the raids on which Norman Lee flew was offset by the failure of others. Almost to the very end, the enemy was tenacious, the battle unrelenting, the losses of aircraft and crews grim.

The above comments are intended to set Norman Lee's aircrew service into the perspective of the air war as a whole. Another observation at a more individual level may be worth making. As Norman Lee remarks in his narrative, all Bomber Command aircrews, especially perhaps those of the four-engined bombers, tended to believe that the aircraft type they flew was the best. That they did so was doubtless an important morale factor. A comparison between the percentage losses of Lancasters, Halifaxes and Stirlings respectively on Norman Lee's operations, however, may be a more reliable indicator of who was right in this particular argument.

End

Also published by Woodfield...
The following titles are all available in high-quality softback format

RAF HUMOUR

Bawdy Ballads & Dirty Ditties of the RAF • A huge collection of the bawdy songs and rude recitations with which RAF personnel would entertain one-another in off-duty hours in WW2. Sure to amuse any RAF veteran. (uncensored – strictly adults only!) *"Not for the frail, the frightfully posh or proper gels – but great fun for everyone else!"* **£9.95**

Upside Down Nothing on the Clock • Dozens of jokes and anecdotes contributed by RAF personnel from AC2s to the top brass... one of our best sellers. *"Highly enjoyable."* **£6.00**

Upside Down Again! • Our second great collection of RAF jokes, funny stories and anecdotes – a great gift for those with a high-flying sense of humour! *"Very funny indeed."* **£6.00**

Was It Like This For You? • A feast of humorous reminiscences & cartoons depicting the more comical aspects of life in the RAF. *"Will bring back many happy memories. Highly recommended."* **£6.00**

I Have Control • former RAF Parachute instructor **Edward Cartner** humorously recalls the many mishaps, blunders and faux-pas of his military career. *Superb writing; very amusing indeed.* **£9.95**

Who is in Charge Here...? • Former RAF Parachute instructor **Edward Cartner** regales us with more inglorious moments from the latter part of his military career as a senior officer. *Superb writing; very amusing indeed.* **£9.95**

MILITARY MEMOIRS & HISTORIES – THE POST-WAR PERIOD

A History of the King's Flight & The Queen's Flight • An illustrated history of the RAF's Royal illustrious squadron, responsible for the air transport of the Royal family from its inception in 1936 to its disbandment in 1995. **£15.00**

Flying the Waves • **Richard Pike** describes his eventful second career as a commercial helicopter pilot, which involved coastguard Air/Sea Rescue operations in the Shetlands and North Sea. **£9.95**

From Port T to RAF Gan • The history of the RAF's most deserted outpost is comprehensively and entertainingly charted by **Peter Doling**, a former RAF officer who served on Gan in the 1970s. Many photos, some in colour. **£20.00**

Korea: We Lived They Died • Former soldier with Duke of Wellington's Regt **Alan Carter** reveals the appalling truth of front-line life for British troops in this now forgotten war. *Very funny in places too.* **£9.95**

Meteor Eject! • Former 257 Sqn pilot [1950s] **Nick Carter** recalls the early days of RAF jets and his many adventures flying Meteors, including one very lucky escape via a Martin-Baker ejector seat... **£9.95**

Pluck Under Fire • Eventful Korean War experiences of **John Pluck** with the Middlesex Regiment. **£9.95**

Return to Gan • Michael Butler's light-hearted account of life at RAF Gan in 1960 and the founding of 'Radio Gan'. Will delight those who also served at this remote RAF outpost in the Indian Ocean. **£12.00**

The Spice of Flight • Former RAF pilot **Richard Pike** delivers a fascinating account of flying Lightnings, Phantoms and later helicopters with 56, 43(F) & 19 Sqns in the RAF of the 1960s & 70s. **£9.95**

Tread Lightly into Danger • Bomb-disposal expert **Anthony Charlwood**'s experiences in some of the world's most dangerous hotspots (Kuwait, Iraq, Lebanon, Somalia, etc) over the last 30 years. **£9.95**

MILITARY MEMOIRS & HISTORIES – WORLD WAR 1 & 2

A Bird Over Berlin Former Lancaster pilot with 61 Sqn **Tony Bird DFC** tells a remarkable tale of survival against the odds during raids on the German capital & as a POW. *"An incredible-but-true sequence of events."* **£9.95**

Algiers to Anzio with 72 & 111 Squadrons Former engineer officer **Greggs Farish**'s diary and photos are a superb historical record of RAF squadron life during Operation 'Husky' – the invasion of Sicily/Italy in 1943. **£9.95**

An Erk's-Eye View of World War 2 • former 'instrument basher' **Ted Mawdsley** salutes the work of the RAF ground crews of WW2, who played a vital role in keeping the RAF's aircraft flying in often adverse conditions. **£9.95**

An Illustrated History of RAF Waddington Former crewmember of the famous Battle of Britain flight Ray Leach has researched the wartime history of this important RAF base. Many photos. *"A superb achievement."* **£20.00**

A Lighter Shade of Blue • A former Radar Operator **Reg O'Neil** recalls his WW2 service in Malta and Italy with 16004 AMES – a front-line mobile radar unit. *'Interesting, informative and amusing.'* **£9.95**

A Shilling's Worth of Promises • Delightfully funny memoirs of **Fred Hitchcock**, recalling his years as an RAF airman during the war and later amusing escapades in the UK and Egypt. *A very entertaining read.* **£9.95**

Beaufighters BOAC & Me • WW2 Beaufighter navigator **Sam Wright** served a full tour with 254 Sqn and was later seconded to BOAC on early post-war overseas routes. *'Captures the spirit of the mighty Beaufighter'* **£9.95**

Carried on the Wind • **Sean Feast** tells the fascinating story of Ted Manners, a 'special duties operator' with 101 Squadron, whose job was to 'spoof' enemy radar and intercept their surface-to-air radio messages in WW2. **£9.95**

Coastal Command Pilot • Former Hudson pilot **Ted Rayner**'s outstanding account of his unusual WW2 Coastal Command experiences, flying in the Arctic from bases in Iceland and Greenland. **£9.95**

Cyril Wild: The Tall Man Who Never Slept • **James Bradley**'s biography of a remarkable Japanese-speaking British Army officer who helped many POWs survive at Sonkurai Camp on the infamous Burma railway. **£9.95**

Desert War Diary • **John Walton**'s diary and photos record the activities of the Hurricanes and personnel of 213 Squadron during WW2 in Cyprus and Egypt. *"Informative and entertaining."* **£9.95**

Espionage Behind the Wire • former POW **Howard Greville** tells the fascinating story of how he worked as a spy for British intelligence (MI6) from inside a German POW camp. **£9.95**

From Fiji to Balkan Skies • Spitfire/Mustang pilot **Dennis McCaig** recalls eventful WW2 operations over the Adriatic/Balkans with 249 Sqn in 43/44. *'A rip-roaring real-life adventure, splendidly written.'* **£9.95**

Get Some In! • The many wartime adventures of **Mervyn Base**, a WW2 RAF Bomb Disposal expert **£9.95**

Hunt Like a Tiger • **Tom Docherty** an illustrated history of 230 squadron – equipped during the war with Sunderland flying boats which were put to many uses in many theatres of war. A fascinating piece of RAF history. **£9.95**

Just a Survivor • Former Lancaster navigator **Phil Potts** tells his remarkable tale of survival against the odds in the air with 103 Sqn and later as a POW. *'An enlightening and well written account.'* **£9.95**

Memoirs of a 'Goldfish' • The eventful wartime memoirs of former 115 Sqn Wellington pilot **Jim Burtt-Smith**, now president of the Goldfish Club - exclusively for aviators who have force-landed into water. **£9.95**

Nobody Unprepared • The history of No 78 Sqn RAF is told in full for the first time by **Vernon Holland** in this absorbing account of the Whitley/Halifax squadron's World War 2 exploits. Full statistics and roll of honour. **£14.95**

No Brylcreem, No Medals • RAF MT driver **Jack Hambleton** 's splendid account of his wartime escapades in England, Shetlands & Middle East blends comic/tragic aspects of war in uniquely entertaining way. **£9.95**

Nobody's Hero • Former RAF Policeman **Bernard Hart-Hallam**'s extraordinary adventures with 2TAF Security Section on D-Day and beyond in France, Belgium & Germany. *"Unique and frequently surprising."* **£9.95**

Operation Pharos • **Ken Rosam** tells the story of the RAF's secret bomber base/staging post on the Cocos Keeling islands during WW2 and of many operations from there. *'A fascinating slice of RAF history.'* **£9.95**

Over Hell & High Water • WW2 navigator **Les Parsons** survived 31 ops on Lancasters with 622 Sqn, then went on to fly Liberators in Far East with 99 Sqn. *'An exceptional tale of 'double jeopardy'.* **£9.95**

Pacifist to Glider Pilot • The son of Plymouth Brethren parents, **Alec Waldron** renounced their pacifism and went on to pilot gliders with the Glider Pilot Regiment at both Sicily & Arnhem. *Excellent photos.* **£9.95**

Pathfinder Force Balkans • Pathfinder F/Engineer **Geoff Curtis** saw action over Germany & Italy before baling out over Hungary. He was a POW in Komarno, Stalags 17a & 17b. *'An amazing catalogue of adventures.'* **£9.95**

Per Ardua Pro Patria • Humour and tragedy are interwoven in these unassuming autobiographical observations of **Dennis Wiltshire**, a former Lancaster Flight Engineer who later worked for NASA. **£9.95**

Ploughs, Planes & Palliasses • Entertaining recollections of RAF pilot **Percy Carruthers**, who flew Baltimores in Egypt with 223 Squadron and was later a POW at Stalag Luft 1 & 6. **£9.95**

RAF/UXB The Story of RAF Bomb Disposal • Stories contributed by wartime RAF BD veterans that will surprise and educate the uninitiated. *"Amazing stories of very brave men."* **£9.95**

Railway to Runway • Wartime diary & letters of Halifax Observer **Leslie Harris** – killed in action with 76 Sqn in 1943 – poignantly capture the spirit of the wartime RAF in the words of a 20-year-old airman. **£9.95**

Seletar Crowning Glory • The history of the RAF base in Singapore from its earliest beginnings, through the golden era of the flying-boats, its capture in WW2 and on to its closure in the 1970s. **£15.00**

The RAF & Me • Former Stirling navigator **Gordon Frost** recalls ops with 570 Sqn from RAF Harwell, including 'Market-Garden' 'Varsity' and others. *'A salute to the mighty Stirling and its valiant crews.'* £9.95

Training for Triumph • **Tom Docherty**'s very thorough account of the amazing achievement of RAF Training Command, who trained over 90,000 aircrew during World War 2. *'An impressively detailed book.'* £12.00

To Strive and Not to Yield • An inspiring account of the involvement of No 626 Squadron RAF Bomber Command in the 'Battle of Berlin' (1943/44) and a salute to the men and women who served on the squadron. £14.95

Un Grand Bordel • Geoffrey French relates air-gunner **Norman Lee**'s amazing real-life adventures with the French Maquis (Secret Army) after being shot down over Europe. *"Frequently funny and highly eventful."* £9.95

UXB Vol 2 • More unusual and gripping tales of bomb disposal in WW2 and after. £9.95

Wot! No Engines? • Alan Cooper tells the story of military gliders in general and the RAF glider pilots who served on Operation Varsity in 1945 in particular. A very large and impressive book with many photos. £18.00

While Others Slept • Former Hampden navigator **Eric Woods** tells the story of Bomber Command's early years and how he completed a tour of duty with 144 Squadron. *'Full of valuable historical detail.'* £9.95

WOMEN & WORLD WAR TWO

A WAAF at War • Former MT driver **Diana Lindo**'s charming evocation of life in the WAAF will bring back happy memories to all those who also served in World War 2. *"Nostalgic and good-natured."* £9.95

Corduroy Days • Warm-hearted and amusing recollections of **Josephine Duggan-Rees**'s wartime years spent as a Land Girl on farms in the New Forest area. *"Funny, nostalgic and very well written."* £9.95

Ernie • **Celia Savage**'s quest to discover the truth about the death of her father, an RAF Halifax navigator with 149 Sqn, who died in WW2 when she was just 6 years old. *"A real-life detective story."* £9.95

In My Father's Footsteps • **Pat Bienkowski**'s moving account of her trip to Singapore & Thailand to visit the places where her father and uncle were both POW's during WW2. £9.95

Lambs in Blue • **Rebecca Barnett's** revealing account of the wartime lives and loves of a group of WAAFs posted to the tropical paradise of Ceylon. *"A highly congenial WW2 chronicle."* £9.95

Radar Days • Delightful evocation of life in the wartime WAAF by former Radar Operator **Gwen Arnold**, who served at Bawdsey Manor RDF Station, Suffolk. *"Amusing, charming and affectionate."* £9.95

Searching in the Dark • The amusing wartime diary of **Peggy Butler** a WAAF radar operator 1942-1946 – written when she was just 19 yrs old and serving at Bawdsey RDF station in Suffolk £9.95

Tales of a Bomber Command Waaf (and her horse) • very entertaining book composed mainly of wartime letters received and sent by **Sylvia Pickering**, who served as a Waaf at RAF Cottesmore and RAF Coningsby. £9.95

More Tales of a Bomber Command Waaf (and her horse) • The second part of **Sylvia Pickering**'s war was spent at RAF Coningsby and HQ 5 Group (Bomber Command) at Morton Hall. Many more entertaining reminiscences. £9.95

Why Did We Join? • In this entertaining book **Eileen Smith** recalls the camaraderie, excitement and heartbreak of working as a Waaf at an operational Bomber Command Station – RAF East Kirkby in Lincolnshire. £9.95

MEMOIRS & HISTORIES – NON-MILITARY

A Beat Around the Bush • **Alastair Tompkins** recounts a variety of his extraordinary experiences– many of them very amusing indeed – as a Bush Policeman in British Colonial Kenya, 1952-62. Very entertaining. £9.95

20th Century Farmers Boy • Sussex farmer **Nick Adames** looks back on a century of rural change and what it has meant to his own family and the county they have farmed in for 400 years. £9.95

Call an Ambulance! • former ambulance driver **Alan Crosskill** recalls a number of light-hearted episodes from his eventful career in the 1960s/70s. *'Very amusing and entertaining'.* £9.95

Harry – An Evacuee's Story • The misadventures of **Harry Collins** – a young lad evacuated from his home in Stockport UK to Manitoba, Canada in WW2. *'An educational description of the life of an evacuee'* £9.95

Just Visiting • Charming and funny book by former Health Visitor **Molly Corbally**, who brilliantly depicts colourful characters and entertaining incidents from her long career. £9.95

Occupation Nurse • **Peter & Mary Birchenall** pay tribute to the achievement of the group of untrained nurses who provided healthcare at Guernsey's only hospital during the German occupation of 1940-45. **£9.95**

The JFK Assassination: Dispelling the Myths • Prepare to revise everything you thought you knew about the most famous assassination of the 20th Century. British historian **Mel Ayton** examines the many 'myths' that have grown up in the 40 years since JFK was murdered and debunks them all. You may be surprised at his conclusions. **£9.95**

FICTION

A Trace of Calcium by **David Barnett** • A commuter comes to the aid of a young woman in trouble, becomes implicated in murder and must use all his resources to clear his name. (contains sex & violence) **£9.95**

Double Time by **David Barnett** • A light-hearted time-travel fantasy in which a bookmaker tries to use a time machine to make his fortune and improve his love-life with hilarious consequences. (contains sex & violence) **£9.95**

Dust & Fury by **David Barnett** • An epic family saga set in the Sultanate of Oman, featuring the lives and loves of an Omani family during the bitter war that led to the foundation of modern Oman. (contains sex & violence) **£15.00**

The Brats • this very entertaining novel by **Tony Paul** is based on the true story of his grandfather, who as a boy along with several friends, stowed away on a ship bound for Canada. The youngsters' brutal mistreatment at the hands of the Captain and Mate of the ship caused a scandal that made headlines in Victorian times. **£9.95**

The Cherkassy Incident by **Hunter Carlyle** Terrorists plot to steal nuclear missiles from a sunken Russian nuclear submarine; can an international team of security agents stop them? (contains sex & violence) **£9.95**

BOOKS FEATURING THE SOUTH COAST & THE SOUTH DOWNS REGION

A Portrait of Slindon • **Josephine Duggan Rees** has written a charming history of this attractive and well-preserved West Sussex village, from its earliest beginnings to the present day, taking in the exploits of its many notable residents over the years. Very informative and entertaining. Illustrated with many photos, some in colour. **£14.95**

Retribution • **Mike Jupp** has created an outrageous and very funny comedy/fantasy novel for adults and older children, featuring bizarre goings-on in a fictional quiet English seaside town that bears a striking resemblance to Mike's home town of Bognor Regis. Brilliantly illustrated. *One of the funniest books you will ever read.* **£9.95**

Unknown to History and Fame • **Brenda Dixon**'s charming portrait of Victorian life in the West Sussex village of Walberton via the writings of Charles Ayling, a resident of the village, whose reports on local events were a popular feature in *The West Sussex Gazette* over many years during the Victorian era. **£9.95**

A Little School on the Downs • **Mary Bowmaker** tells the amazing story of Harriet Finlay-Johnson, headmistress of a little village school in Sompting, West Sussex in the 1890s, whose ideas and classroom techniques began a revolution in education. She also scandalised society at the time by marrying a former pupil, 20 years her junior. **£9.95**

The South Coast Beat Scene of the 1960s The South Coast may not have been as famous as Liverpool in the swinging sixties but it was nevertheless a hotbed of musical activity. Broadcaster **Mike Read** traces the complete history of the musicians, the fans and the venues from Brighton to Bognor in this large and lavishly-illustrated book. **£24.95**

Boys & Other Animals • **Josephine Duggan Rees's** warm-hearted and delightfully funny account of a mother's many trials and tribulations bringing up a boisterous all-male family on a farm in rural Sussex during the 1950s-70s. **£9.95**

Woodfield books are available direct from the publishers by mail order

Telephone your orders to (**+44** if outside UK) **01243** 821234

Fax orders your to (**+44** if outside UK) **01243** 821757

Write to: Book Orders, Woodfield Publishing, Bognor Regis, West Sussex PO21 5EL

All major credit cards accepted Please make cheques payable to 'Woodfield Publishing'.

Visit our website for up-to-date details of our latest titles and special offers. Secure online purchasing is also available

at: **www.woodfieldpublishing.com**

Full money-back guarantee: If you are not satisfied with any of our books, simply return them to us in good condition and we will refund your money, no questions asked.